The Unfinished Symphony Conductor

"Hark, hark, you're rocking the ark."

The Unfinished Symphony Conductor

by

Don Gillis

with
illustrations
by
William Foge

Austin : The Pemberton Press : 1967

Introduction

I have known Don Gillis for over 300 moons and have enjoyed in that time his company, his musicianship and his prose writing (sic), and I am confident that those of you who take up this book will be able to put it down only if you do so during my introduction. If you should put the book down because you are laughing so hard you drop it, that's your problem and doesn't count.

Don Gillis is one of those rare human beings who has steadfastly refused to allow the world to pin a label on him. For one thing what label would you pin? He is a conductor, a teacher, a broadcast producer, an excellent composer and probably unfinished philosopher, but most of all he is an indisputable human being whose willingness to share his sense of humor fashions him into a weird sort of philanthropist (another label that won't stick either because it will fall off while he chuckles about the idea of wearing it.) Read on.

Hugh Downs

Proclamations and Pacifiers

There were several busy helpers on this zestful journey, some actual living human beings, and the rest frictional (such as the typewriter eraser which I have used since my sophomore days at Texas Christian University). A certain secretary (who thought that shorthand was when people had stumpy fingers) was trusted with the task of sprinkling the commas in at more or less regular intervals, comma. She is no longer with me.

I owe a small debt of gratitude to the inventor of the parenthetical phrase (which I acknowledge thusly), and I am obliged to the team of Smith and Corona for the use of their typewriter keys. I became especially fond of their margin-release mechanism which allowed me extra freedom in marginal areas. I am also grateful to the prepositions "at," "to," "from" and "with," none of which look the worse for wear at having been dangled so frequently throughout. Whatever footnotes there are have been supplied by the pedal division of the Conn Organ Company of Elkhart, Indiana, and Webster's Dictionary (which I borrowed to improve my diction) has now been returned to its rightful owner, a certain Charley Webster of Requiem, Mass.

Medical terms used in this book were picked up while listening to the firm of Drs. Ted and Warren Cline, who also kept me in reasonable health (at least physically) during its gestation period at what they led me to believe were fair prices.

The material in this book was taken from a series of lectures which were hopefully planned to be (but not) given at Harvard, Yale, Princeton, Waxahachie Institute of Technology, and the Eastman School of Music.

I would also like to express my appreciation to the employees of the bar at the Park Place Hotel in Traverse City, Michigan, for aiding me in deciphering my scribblings after they had gotten soggy through the carelessness of a friend of mine, a certain Jack Daniels (who shall be nameless). Jack also came into New York to help me finish the book in case he has been missed lately around Lynchburg, Tennessee.

The chapter numbers ("I" through "XIII") were supplied courtesy of the Roman Empire and the words "The End" are direct quotes from one of the most interesting parts of *Little Women*.

The term "Caution" (which I frequently use to adjure people with) was leased from the Tarrant County, Texas Highway Department, which also loaned me "Soft Shoulders," but I couldn't think of a clean way to use it.

I also want to thank Neil Kjos, Sr., a music publisher of note who, in a fit of uncontrolled loquaciousness, once suggested to me that I should write a book about conducting. This will probably make him want to give up talking altogether. At least to me.

Other than these things and people, I can't seem to think of anything else to express my appreciation at.

> Don Gillis,
> Traverse City, Michigan, and
> Riverdale, New York,
> 1962, '63, '64, '65, and '66.
> (I write slow.)

CHAPTER I

Genesis

Hark!

I have always liked that word somehow or other and I'm sorry it isn't in common usage anymore much. It means "listen" or "pay attention," and I have used it here so that you, my students, would "hearken unto my words" (as the prophets used to utter in the olden days). It is a neat word, even if it is considered archaic these days (we can't eat archaic and have it, too, you know)—anyway, I'm sure that Noah must have shouted "hark" a time or so on his trip with the animals, especially when the elephants and giraffes and kangeroos got to horsing around.

"Hark, hark, you're rocking the ark!," he probably shouted, and he wasn't happy at all until the dove brought back—yes, you've guessed it—a twig. This showed the deluge was over, and he let all of the animals out two by two (except the rabbits, as they had begat the entire voyage). And although the Bible doesn't come right out and say so, I think Noah kept that twig as a souvenir of what was the very first excursion into batonistics—a conducted tour.

So you see how logical it was for succeeding generations to use the same sort of thing as scepters or symbols (especially if they wanted to succeed in their generation). Such things were the signs of their times and in conducting there are a lot of kinds of times for which there are signs that I am sure we are bound to take up later as part of our helpfulness toward you.

I hope this friendly little allegory sets the tone for our educational excursion (musically speaking) and that it doesn't rock the ark too much. The tone we are setting is "A-440," by the way, and the voyage you are taking is into the land of the Goliaths who tell little David how to play on his harp.

From here on out, I want you to bring your pitchpipe to class, although don't light it in here as I can't stand the acrid odor of burning pitch. I would prefer, instead, that you bring a tuning fork (sterling, if possible) as we might just all want to stand up and sing our Alma Mater hymn for this seminar in twig-twitching, which I'm sure you all know as "We are bound for the Promised Land!" After today, however, leave your halos in the cloakroom, as we take up gestures later and I wouldn't want you to bend them, unless, of course, your career is already insured or subsidized by a wealthy and solvent foundation, father, or friend.

So then, when I say "Hark!," that's just what I mean and so do it! Let's get it straight right here and now who's teaching this course! Which (after I've harked at you) leaves you nothing to do but "hearken" back and take notes as you go along. Just don't take any of mine, however, as composers have a rough enough time finding any good ones left, especially after Beethoven and that bunch used most of the better ones up.

Just follow my instructions as we go from Alpha to Omega (by way of Carnegie Hall and Lincoln Center) about all of this, and you will join the ranks of the greatly blessed whose twigs have triumphed triumphantly. So, then, doth the history of the mystery of men who mold music unravel itself.

So hark! For thus beginneth the reading!

*   *   *

So that we may more rapidly get this matter down to its basic basics, will you please all turn to pages 210 and 211 of the Webster's Collegiate Dictionary, Fifth Edition, where we will find the definition of "to conduct" and "conductor" in its native habitat. Please note that I am editing Webster slightly, as he does go on and on about a subject once he gets his teeth into it. We will take up the verb "to conduct" first, and I quote:

"The act or method of leading; of guidance; to transmit, as in

Sometimes conductors have different titles such as "Chef d'Orchestre."

*If you are English then you don't have to do anything
except drink tea and trumpets. Or is it crumpets?*

heat; or an act or manner of carrying on." I interrupt here momentarily to say that we will point out much about this latter phrase later. Mr. Webster then, after several intervening words, finally gets around to the conductor himself:

"A conductor (the Fifth Edition reveals) is one who performs or executes a symphony." Later we can all look up "execute" and see what *that* means. Or, the conductor is something that "acts as a conductor," and then Webster goes on to mention heat and electricity, which is purely irrelevant since the word "to act"—which implies footlights and applause and names in big letters on billboards—is the word underlined in *my* dictionary. Whether Mr. Webster did this personally or had someone do it for him is a matter for debate. I imagine by the time he got down to the Fifth Edition he was probably hiring his own help, as I understand this book has been a smash hit for years. But I digress.

He concludes with the statement, succinct and to the point, that a conductor is "A guide, as of travelers." There are some other things in Italics, too, but I'm much safer in French or Spanish and so won't take a chance on losing anything by attempting an off-the-cuff translation here.

Sometimes conductors have different titles, such as "Director" or "Chef d'Orchestre" (that latter term is a foreign phrase and it is always good to throw in something like this now and then to show you're a worldly character). It simply means "cook of the orchestra" and if you care to practice in front of a mirror, put on one of those tall white chef hats and beat time with a ladle until you get that foreign feeling or until someone in a white jacket removes you gently to the nearest Home for the Bewildered. But no matter what you are called (and there are unprintable items I've heard conductors called that the editors won't even allow in a glossary of terms, much less in a family book like this) . . . no matter what you are called, YOU are the leader and there just wouldn't BE any music at all if it weren't for YOU!

That's Rule No. 1, students, so memorize it and then chew it up quickly and swallow it so that you can not only digest the truth of it, but so that no one will ever find it on you in case you get searched.

I learned this trick once from an ex-Scotland Yard inspector who worked near the Custom's Office on the Mexican side at Juarez helping people swallow their about-to-be-confiscated bottled contraband. One night at the heighth of his fame, I saw him put away a full quart of tequila, bottle and all, and after serving a short term charged with Biopsy, he made a fortune when he was signed by Prison Records who made his "Contraband" music even more popular than their "Sing Along at Sing-Sing" platters had been. But I have digressed again.

There is one last thing that I should mention about names while we are still all together, and this concerns your own name. It should be a good-sounding name, one that hints of dignity and power, and if you can figure out a way to translate it into a foreign language, you're already a little ahead of the game. People just don't take to names for conductors like Richard Roe and John Doe (these are great on check samples but not for much else), but the general public does seem to have a tendency to put more stock in something like "Xerxes Berserkson" or "Julio di Herbavox." Don't hesitate to change your name to something more fanciful than the one you were born with if you think it will help your career. This isn't deceitful—women do it all the time, and in these days of equal rights, what could be equaler?

Warning: if your name is already something foreign-sounding like Mynheer Gimple or Aram Skarouhm, for heaven's sakes leave things as they are and don't get carried away and change it to something as plebian as John Doe or Richard Roe or you'll end up as a check sample instead of being world-famously world-famous.

Of course, if you're lucky enough to be English and have a first name like "Sir" or (in the case of Byron), "Lord," then you don't have to do anything except wear your Eton tie and drink tea and trumpets. Or is it crumpets? Unfortunately for those of us who are born in the land of the free and the home of the brave, the only royalty titles we have are those like the "King of Jazz," the "Sultan of Swing," and the "Duke of Ellington." And they are all taken. But let this not deter you, for as someone or other once said, "A rose by any other name, and so forth."

We are faced with problems of greater magnitude. So let us

assume that the world not only needs conductors, but more specifically, the world needs YOU as its conductor. I'm sorry that blinding lights from heaven and kings with knighting swords have gone out of style; otherwise, there would be no doubt about who the anointed really are. Lacking these specific evidences of your calling, however, a self-proclaimed appointment will have to suffice and if you proclaim loudly enough, everyone will notice you. They may not like you, but they *will* notice you.

And don't just casually mention that you are taking up conducting like it was something like Croquet or U-2 over-flying, either. Wander around the campus (we presume you are in school, but if you're not, find a campus to wander around so that people will think you are) (which is almost as good as being and not half as expensive)—wander around with a sort of lost look on your face as if your inner thoughts have just taken over and you are now wrestling with your soul. This will accomplish two things: first, your facial muscles will freeze into a position of strained thinking (which is always good if you are a conductor) and also, someone will finally get around to asking you what is wrong.

"Sylvester" they will say, "what the hell is rocking your ark these days?"

It is at this moment in time that you can shout (with all of the zest of a galloping Paul Revere) that you have been "called" to the podium. Do this in the same reverent style of a preacher announcing his own "call" to the pulpit and before the day is over, the news will spread all over school that YOU have been called (and not even collect!) to be a conductor.

The very fact that you will admit to such a thing immediately raises your status and from that moment on you can be excused from almost any normal neuroticism such as attending classes regularly. Be misunderstood, if you can, for that also focuses attention on you. I must say in passing here, however, that composers usually have the edge on you in this sort of thing. For they are also "called" and set apart and they go around looking for posterity as if somebody had just offered a reward for finding it. You, on the other hand, are only looking for a podium. And so therefore (and probably whereas) this series of lectures sprang, like Phoenix, from the ashes of my own unfulfilled career. (be sure to see Chapter II.)

Because conducting (or wafting the wand) has such a magical meaning in these latter days of music, I would be remiss if I didn't set down some historical facts about the whole history of this gentle craft.

The pages of history crackle with sizzle-like sounds as music reviews itself in print. We learn, for example, that in the yore days, music used to be led (or guided) by a fellow who sat at a harpsichord in the middle of his ensemble. This was back in the days when the harpsichord played the figured bass (which is a sort of musical quarterbacking involving Roman numerals pertaining to chords—the "note" kind, not the harpsi-), and the fellow playing it could do that and still have time enough to get some order organized out of the confusion caused by the other guys who played things like lutes, bombards, serpents, oliphants, and sackbuts. These latter instruments are "avis rara" (rare birds) these days except among such fringe-area *afficiandos* as musicologists, so we can't suggest that you take up harpsichord as a pre-requisite to your career.

For those of you who may be vague about the harpsichord itself, let me say that it is the sort of instrument you might come out with if you were trying to build a piano but didn't quite have the hang of it yet. It gives off a tinkling sort of sound, as if a hummingbird's wings had brushed against a delicate lace handkerchief which had suddenly been turned into purest gold (or like the pleasant tinkling tones caused by ice-cubes swizzling in the bubbles of bourbon and soda at high tide). There was another similar instrument called the "clavichord." I could never remember the difference until someone told me that the strings on a harpsichord were "plucked" (as one might pluck a harp, or even a chicken), while the clavichord was only "clavved." I remember that of the two of them, the clavichord was the most well-tempered.

Harpsichords are not very loud, which is why they are among the few remaining instruments known to modern civilization which have not been put into the marching band at football games. You

Announce that YOU have been called (and not even "collect") to be conductor!

I don't want any students of mine in a state of mental untidiness.

may have thought I was digressing again, but I assure you that I mentioned this not only to demonstrate my own vast resources of knowledge, but also to have you ready in case somebody ever asks you what a harpsichord is. I don't want any students of mine to be caught up in a state of mental untidiness. Ever!

After the harpsichord "sitting-stance" for conductors, some of the more outgoing of the group got to standing up during the performance and waving rolled-up paper around in order to keep the various sections co-ordinated. It has been said by one ancient writer: "For best results, roll ye up some money which ye musicians will watch fervently, forsaking even their jots and tittles in an effort to be attentive unto ye leader." Actually since I am the old ancient (in person) whom I was quoting, then you'd better believe it, as remember what I said about "hark" earlier and who's teaching this class. Even if it isn't a hundred per cent right, all I can say is that *if* there was any money to be waved, it would have been ye *leaders* and not ye *sidemen* who had it. Even as of today, *n'est-ce pas?* (meaning: "right, fellows?"). See how you can work these foreign terms in and really get that international flavor? Jet jargon, it's called!

Waving sheaves of music paper (or money) as a scent for the musicians to follow became more and more common as the size of the orchestra grew. And soon conductors began standing up and gesticulating hither, thither, and yon, beckoning (with all of their might and main) the musicians onward so they could all hit the cadences at roughly the same time. These gesticulators faced the audience while waving, too. I don't know who finally got them turned around the other way, but it was smart thinking. Finally the orchestras got so big that all of the harpsichord players decided that (since they couldn't be heard in the general din of oliphant trumpeters, lute twangers, and bombard blasters anyway) they would just get up on a box and really take over.

Now it is not recounted in history who it was that invented the podium (or box) upon which conductors stand, but you'll have to admit that it was a pretty good idea. For if there's one sure way of getting looked up to, it's to stand up on a box while the looker-uppers are sitting down. Next to the invention of the wheel, I would say that the podium was the most significant step upward for civilization to take, and it's a shame that the names of both of these fellows are shrouded in the mystery of forgotten time. If I were a sculptor, I would make up a symbolic statue with a big wheel on a podium and dedicate the whole thing to Sir Isaac Newton, who first foresaw the gravity of the situation.

The rolled-up paper stage of conducting didn't last too long, and so new and more effective materials were experimented with. One story has it that the orchestra leaders of the time of the French composer, Jean-Baptiste Lully, used a rather sizeable staff or gilded pole (not the ten-foot kind which you would use to not touch something with—these were more like gold-plated billiard cues). This same story has it that Lully himself was conducting a concert, beating time on the floor with this club to keep the boys together, when he smashed it down on his foot during a *forte* passage and gangrene not only set in, but rigor and mortis soon joined him. This is the first time in music history that anyone ever crushed himself into immortality with his own downbeat. However, he died rich, and that's some comfort—but you can bet your Grove's Dictionary of Music that he didn't make it just writing music. He made it by conducting, thus proving for all time that the pen is not either as mighty as the sword *or* the baton, no matter what the poets say.

Berlioz and Mendelssohn were superb conductors (as those of us who read legends are prone to know), and there is one story that I've heard every year since 1915 as if it had just been archived out right along with the Dead Sea Scrolls. It seems that both of these fine fellows were finally to meet, and a ceremony was arranged for them to pay tribute to each other by exchanging batons. Berlioz had one made up with gold inlay and solid ivory that was pretty expensive even for those times, and presented it to Mendelssohn with a flowery speech which freely translated meant, "use it in good health."

Mendelssohn responded with a flowery speech also, but when Berlioz unwrapped *his* present, he became furious because all *he* saw was a withered-looking twig. And, as the legend keeps on saying, he walked out in a huff, not realizing that the twig was in reality a piece of laurel—symbolic of greatest achievement among the ancient Greeks. There's no real point to this story except that you might pass it along sometime when you're out to dinner and there's a lull in the conversation.

Tschaikowsky (Peter Illich) (1840-1893) was another composer who used to fool around some with conducting. His problem was, though, that he kept thinking his head was going to come off during the performance and so he used to stand up there holding it on with one hand and beating time with the other. Now, many a conductor has lost his head (or at least his place) during a performance, but, if you feel like this is going to happen to you too often, take up some other profession unless you're three-handed. Conducting is no easy occupation, you know, and so if you're going into it you just have to be prepared to take what comes, whether it's losing your head or clobbering your metatarsal bones.

Franz Liszt was still another composer who used to conduct, and not only that, he wore expensive white kid gloves while doing so. And after the concert he would acknowledge his applause by taking them off (his gloves) and throwing them to the audience as souvenirs. Actually people collected a lot of things of his as souveniers, even his cigar butts as he was very popular. There is a story I once read about an elderly dowager in England, which—while seemingly unbelievable, was printed in a first-class magazine whose credulity is not to be doubted, and so therefore I pass it along to you as a brand of gospel that only the English can print in their highly credible magazines (and if we can't believe the English, whom can we believe these days when the entire world seems helter-skeltering to dismals and disasters?).

Anyway (to continue) this ancient dowager died and after her death, two of Liszt's castaway cigar butts were found (tissue paper wrapped) tucked into her bosom. For me this was the height of fame and I took up smoking just on this account. However, I must admit to failure so far, for although I have peered down many a bodice in research, I have never found a single one of my used cigarettes even, much less a cigar butt. But (as Hendrick Hudson said as he gave up looking for the Northwest Passage to India), "That is neither here nor there."

Meanwhile, back in the history of conducting, wild things were happening. The day of the virtuoso conductor arrived in the mid-nineteenth century, and it's still here. And while it is here, we might as well take advantage of the whole deal by joining right in, making for the nearest forest to hack down a mighty oak from which to whittle out a baton, carving out our own future (as it were) as we step upon the throne that rules the kingdom of music. And the last one there is a sissy!

But joining the world's third-oldest profession cannot be a whim, even if we were whimsical enough to want to. It takes skill and preparation and study and courage and determination and friends on the Board of Directors. And first of all, you have to know music!

This is why I am so glad that you have had all the prerequisite courses like rote-songs and note reading. It is a burden off my mind not to have to explain the difference between sharps and flats to you to say nothing of the more complicated gadgets such as repeat signs. This way we can get right down to the basics of your getting a good grip on your ego and standing out in the music school lobby proclaiming yourself to be the "awaited" one. When you do get your feet firmly planted in the middle of that foyer floor, take a strong stand against anything that happens to be conducted by anybody else, but most of all, use the bigger words in musical vocabulary, like "interpretation" and "muscular dystrophy." And wear an air of contempt, too, especially toward mundane things such as mundane things, neo-classism, self-discipline, and other people's opinions. In short, never give the other guy an even break when it comes to talking about yourself. "Every man his own wife" is our motto when it comes to press-agenting ourselves into the limelight. And once this is accomplished, leap like a panther to the nearest orange crate and wave your arms in all directions until enough musicians are mesmerized to play for you, coda and all. Just accept this as truth: if you stand there waving long enough, you'll attract players—if only for their hope that you'll fall off the box so they can get up on it.

Remember that old yarn about Berlioz and Mendelssohn?

Let it not be said that this book does not cover everything!

A summary of this chapter would prove inconclusive to say the least, but we will do it anyway as we want to be consistent throughout. First of all, I promise not to get on the podium during this book except for demonstration purposes only, so you can trust me and call me friend as well as teacher. And secondly, I want to give you what we academicians call your "Syllabus for Success," and your three steps to the podium are taken as follows:

    a. First you have to want to,

    b. Then you got to get to,

    c. And then, don't ever get off!

Follow these rules and long may you wave!

In conclusion (and the end is always justified by the end if our goal is—as is mine—in surging ever onward toward "The End"), I must say that "Any resemblance (in this book) between anyone, living or dead (or in any other state of being, but not necessarily restricted thereto) is purely co-incidental—but, if not, only the innocent have been changed to protect their names."

You have to put things like this in books, folks, to keep from being sued and I hope I'm covered.

But in case I'm not, does anyone know a good defense attorney?

But I digress. On to Chapter II.

Untitled—As Yet

In olden days when teachers wore togas or the like, it was the custom for the students to gather around the professor's feet, as it were, and many a cup of hemlock was merrily quaffed as the students got to know their teachers and even to call them by their first name, like "Soc." In those golden days also, the mentor frequently had the students living in his own home and sopping bread from the same dish of gravy, and while I would not like for us to get that informal (after all, I hardly know you), perhaps you will feel less insecure about the whole arrangement if I speak to you freely on a man-to-man basis. (Please note that this does not apply to the women.) Afterwards, if we get on a first name basis, then you may feel free to call me by mine, "Doc."

Ready?

Once upon a time (as we say in the story-telling business), there was a little boy who lived in a small (but neatly kept) midwestern town near the Missouri River, but not near enough to get flooded when the Big Muddy overflowed its banks. This boy was me, and the town wasn't anywhere near the Missouri River at all, actually—but whoever heard of Brushy Creek?

It was in this town that I saw my first conductor, and he was dressed up in a white uniform and played a gold slide trombone. As far as I recall, he didn't use a baton at all, although I do remember that he pointed at one or more of his players from time to time. And none of them pointed back, either, for he was obviously the boss and

The race to the podium begins the moment a musician is born.

NEVER be a secret beater!

to prove it, he played several of his own compositions including "The Whistler and His Dog," in which a lot of them put down their instruments and whistled and a few of them even barked. He was a powerful man, all right, and I decided when I got big I wanted to wear a white uniform and play a solid gold trombone and make people play my own compositions, too. It was an impressive moment in time.

The preceding paragraph is what us writers call "local color," but what my Dad used to tell me was my tendency toward exaggeration. This was usually called to my attention by the use of a shingle on the seat of my overalls, and I was almost out of high school before I found out that this form of punishment wasn't what the English teacher meant by "syntax." But spank as he did, he never did quite cure me of my dramatization of the truth as I spoke (in what later I learned to be "dialogue"), nor when I got my first fountain pen and started to write things down on paper (usually excuses to my teachers, signing Dad's name). A be-bearded uncle of mine predicted dire things for me and said that I spoke constantly in "whoppers." However, I was not deterred in my desires to make a mark for myself (that same uncle made an "X" for *himself*), and so I wrote a letter in lucid and crystal-clear prose and mailed it away to a soap company to get vast quantities of perfumed hardwater soap which (if I sold more than the other kids) would win me a Shetland pony.

My object here, of course, was to sell the pony once I won it and buy myself a gold slide trombone and a white uniform and go into the band-leading business. But when my furtive efforts at this sort of prose writing were discovered (largely due to the arrival of several cartons filled with the aforementioned soap), Dad got out the shingle again and said that if I ever did anything like that in the future, he would whale me from there to St. Joe. My mother suggested that if I felt I just had to write, I should take up poetry. At least they wouldn't get any perfumed hardwater soap out of that!

But no sooner had I started in on poetry (one of my early ones was a squirrelly little prophetic two-liner about my own conducting career that went:

"I saw the Ocean.

It saw me, too, I think.

At least it waved.")

. . . no sooner had my poetic career started than they decided that maybe I had better go into music, and so the welkin rang to my trombone blasts and Mom knitted herself some earmuffs. They were happy at last! Even people who played the slide trombone were easier to explain than poets were back in those days.

The only reason I have revealed this intimate and little-known part of my life is to point out that I am still prone to exaggerate from time to time and it still might creep into this book now and then. I also wanted to mention that I took up music.

Freud might have something to say about some *syndrome* or other connected with my failure to sublimate my desire to be a conductor, hinting that I got a nasty little psychosis as a result that even the passing years haven't cleared up yet. But it all goes to prove how carefully I've prepared to be able to write a book like this on conducting, and if I am caught straying from the straight and narrow a time or so in these pages it isn't any different than the sign I saw recently on a window of a record store in Ann Arbor, Michigan that was having a sale. It said:

"Ormandy, Munch, and Reiner—40% off!" Heck, my average will be at least as good as that.

Until now I have spent most of my time in the adjacent art of writing music as a certain form of livelihood, a fact documented by several music encyclopedias and a few thousand performances by conductors who have thought that my music was really something to shake a stick at. There is a picture of me somewhere in somebody's old archives or other taken one day when I was sitting in a highchair and wearing what were then called "rompers." In this picture I had one hand upon the piano keys (as if I were even then groping around for a hit tune) and in the other hand I had a firmly-clutched spoon, looking all for the world like I had just successfully completed the finale of the Beethoven 9th as the youngest conductor of all times (including four-four). So it is true that the hand that rocks in the cradle may roll up mighty sounds in later years if he ever finds the proper sized baton and a podium to match.

The mistake most embryonic conductors make is that they don't announce it soon enough. In my own case (even though I gave up conducting later at the request of my mother, who hadn't been able yet to satisfactorily explain to her friends about my being a composer, much less a conductor, too) another existing photograph seems to reveal my inner schemings dramatically.

When I was only five, my brother and I were photographed by an itinerant photographer who owned his own goat. Although the goat didn't figure in the picture (as you paid extra if you used him), he was very much there, for I remember vividly that he ate my brother's stocking cap during the time exposure. It was a cold day and my brother and I were standing beside an old-fashioned water pump, freezing to death, our pearly teeth chattering and our goosebumps burrowing inward, making us look more dimpled than ever all over.

I had the handle of the pump in my hand and he stood there holding a cup, and to this day that picture reminds me of an out-of-work conductor with his agent. A friendly phrenologist who later examined it (along with the bumps on my head as we were planning what I should take in college) said that it sure looked to her like I should be. By this time, however, it was too late, as I had already surpassed Franz Schubert by having three Unfinished Symphonies to his one. I had even written a madrigal once, but it was out of season and the teacher wouldn't let me keep it.

I am relating all of these interesting things only to prove that I could have been a full-time conductor if I hadn't traded in my sharp baton for a dull manuscript pen. Even so, that phrenologist was partly right, for I have (in my fame-infested career) trod on many a podium, and it is from the fullness of this experience that I am willingly transferring the wisdom of the passing years on to you—students now, but *Maestri* of tomorrow.

My own career as a conductor was beset with hazards (as I review it from my dotage), and while I am still alive I would like to go on record that it is a trade that can have some bad after-effects. I remember one engagement I had conducting at a Stock Show and Rodeo in Fort Worth, Texas. My job was to provide music for the various acts on the program, *musicaire* to the multitudes of high-hatted patrons (the horsey set, as it were, only these high hats were Stetsons of the ten gallon kind and the horses were the ones wearing tails).

All of this called for alertness and a tremendous baton technique, for the acts consisted of such things as bronc-busting, brahma bull-dogging, calf-roping, and bareback riding. Now at first glance I realize that one would not imagine that the demands of conducting, say, for a calf-roping act, would compare even in the slightest to the dexterity required for the Firebird Suite or such, yet surprisingly enough, one was constantly challenged to maintain the high standards of the conductor's art as they are made manifest in our modern times. Under ordinary circumstances, the conductor is either in a pit or a podium, but in the case of the Rodeo, one found one's self conducting up near the rafters, at least a hundred yards away from where the acts were performing down on the tanbark (as we call it in rodeo lingo). Not that I'm trying to set up any excuse pattern, but facts are facts, ma'am, no matter whether it's bullfighting in *Carmen* or bull-wrestling in Fort Worth.

I was up to almost all of the demands of Grand Entries and trick roping and such—all, except perhaps, those involving the dancing Palomino.

Now it may well be that not too many of you will ever come up against this problem, but let it not be said that this book does not cover everything. When you conduct for a dancing horse it is necessary to watch that spot just back of the saddle (near the tail), and when that part comes up *you* give a downbeat. This gives the illusion that the horse is keeping time with the music and everyone leaves thinking how smart that animal is, when the real truth is that the dadblamed critter couldn't tell the difference between a waltz and a treble-clef sign unless you helped him. And, of course, the horse is the one who gets all of the applause.

So if you're reluctant about sharing your bows with soloists, don't go in for this sort of musicality. I myself was not only covered with chagrin, but I also got a stubborn form of allergy which the doctor claimed to have been caused by horse hair. I know better though, because I still break out with the hives every time I hear of somebody else getting better notices than I do. Even humans!

The first public performance I ever had of any of my own compositions was one which was ushered into the world by a lady conductor. You don't see too many of these, and since there's something in the book later about them, we won't go into it much right now. Suffice it to say that I thought she did a magnificent job of musical mid-wifery, and even though the opus died later of over-exposure and pre-natal under-nourishment, I shall always be grateful to her for bringing my firstborn score into the world. Even the critic liked it, *although* he did point out a few similarities to Franck, Strauss, Sibelius, Debussy, Tchaikowsky, Berlioz, John Phillip Sousa, and Dixie. Well, at least I was reviewed in print, *although* I never did fully understand his remark about how I reminded him of "Tom Swift and his Eclectic Music-writer."

Since I have interjected these personal notes about my career both on the podium and being heard from it, I might as well confess why I gave it up altogether and therefore can now write about all of this with such clarity and insight.

It happened on a trip to the Orient, for which occasion I had outfitted myself with tails (shades of that horse story again!). Anyway, resplendent in tails and white tie, I skulked around the wings night after night waiting for one of the regular conductors to succumb to beri-beri or some other dread tropical disease. They stayed in remarkably good health, unfortunately, and *although* I finally did get to conduct once, it was in the daytime and I didn't get to wear my dress suit after all.

Somewhere along the way, however (involving a spirit of cunning and intrigue never before known in the annals of international crime), somebody stole my dress-suit trousers and I arrived back in the States with a gorgeous (and unconducted-in) conductor's tailcoat and no pants. And it played havoc with my career, as the only place I could decently accept engagements from then on was in orchestra pits.

But these are reminiscences from my golden past, and while I am sure they have been intensely interesting to all of you, it is of *now* and *your* future that we must speak. Not that this time has been wasted, for it will give each and every one of you a working guide on writing your own memoirs, copies of which you might like to send to me if there is little or no expense involved.

Let us take up *now* first and the *future* later.

Interplanetary exploration being what it is these days, we were bound to find out sooner or later about music among the creatures who inhabit Venus, Mars, and the moon. The music up there uses only the *lines* of the staff, by the way—they're out'er space, remember? This truth was ascertained by one of our astronotes who went just a little high one night when his Van Nuy's radiation belt slipped and he was plummeted straight into a rehearsal hall on Zot, a little-known planet of the fifth galaxy. We are grateful to him for letting us in on the fact that space musicians play only on instruments made out of rubber and since all of us scientists know that rubber is a non-conducting type, just be glad you learned it here. Even in these days of inflation when the quarter note has gone up to thirty-five cents, you are still better off down here among your fellow earth creatures where the problem of integration and disintegration has to be solved first before we can even begin to think of taking up the question of unemployed student conductors.

So my advice to those of you who have been contemplating a career out yonder beyond the wild blue, well—just cancel your reservations at Cape Kennedy. You wouldn't have been happy anyway as space suits don't have tails!

In such turbulent times as these when the world is crying out for leaders, it therefore seemed logical for me to busy myself doing something constructive—and thus this book about my fine-fathered friends, the conductors.

Most of my colleagues (among whom is a retired rajah and a practicing hermit) have gone on record advising me not to write about these leaders for whom (at least according to *them*) (the leaders) the world is crying.

"You" (they say with blanched faces and frightened eyebrows), "You will never get another performance of your immortal music!"

You see, I am a composer and that is why they said that. For they know full well that conductors are to composers as Santa is to Claus. But I over-rode their admonitions because I knew it just HAD to be a book. It couldn't be a picture because the subject was already too wide for existing screens, let alone the predicate. And a book on conducting has been needed for longer than we have needed conductors even.

The author's life is always fraught with danger, and it may well be that my own career will terminate as quickly as did that of another friend of mine named Chester Feathers, whose book "Hiccups and Flying Saucers" was shredded unmercifully not only by science editors everywhere, but by the WTCU as well. After his cremation (I have his ashes at home on the mantle and do wish I could remember to buy an urn) I pledged myself anew to dedicate my efforts to the task of finishing, even if it meant being barred from every concert hall in both the eastern and western hemispheres, as well as elsewhere. And having taken my oath, almost by the time I had finished saying "brave, clean, and reverent," I had finished it and have almost half-a-bucketful of pronouns left over, to say nothing of some extra adverbs.

I had originally started to call this lesson "To Be or Not To Be," but, remembering the dangers of contagious plagiarism and fearful of needing to see an oculist myself for having plagiarized, I desisted, refraining even from calling it "To Beat or Not To Beat." But either title would have illustrated graphically the problem that keeps coming up in the minds of the music school set, which is: "Shall I, or shall I not, become the world's greatest conductor?" And if you think I'm joking, take a poll among musicians and you'll find that most of them believe (if they were given that golden chance) that they could wave that wand with all of the magical results as are currently being achieved by all of the major conductors in the now-known civilized world as we now know it. The race to the podium seems to begin the moment a musician is born—or maybe sooner, remembering Bridey Murphy.

The only exception I have ever heard of was (or were) some Siamese twins from Siam who won their first fame as concert artists playing piano duets—four hands, one stool. A certain P. T. Something-or-other offered them staggering sums to take up conducting, but they refused, preferring to go into the side show business as the hours were better. They did, however, study the baton a bit and later patented it as the back-scratcher with long handles for people with short arms. It is said of them that they also coined the famous showbiz phrase, "You scratch my back and I'll scratch mine," but who knows, it could have been anybody. They later died—but then, we all have to go some way.

It is a truism that *almost* everybody wants to be the man with the baton and this is good, because in spite of the old adage "All work and no play," we do have players in ample multiplicity and if that's all that anybody wanted to do was play, well then, who would lead them? The world is in enough dark despair as it is without bringing up another problem. Composers would be pretty frantic, for who would lead their hits and masterpieces from the wilderness of oblivion if it weren't for conductors?

There was a time in music history when composers were expected to conduct their own creations, but this seems to have gone out of fashion somewhat these days. As a composer I personally believe this is because the Propaganda Division of Conductors, Incorporated has fomented this thought to put down competition, but I can't prove it. The conductors are aided and abetted in this matter by the music critics, too. Which is about the only thing conductors and critics have ever agreed on, ever. We'll probably get around to composers (especially me) again later. And critics, too, no doubt.

You will note that from time to time what you might consider "digressions" creep into this otherwise neatly arranged handbook for the conductor, and lest you think I have just indulged myself in the free fantasy of discursive thinking, let me admit it—if for no other reason than to show you by example how such things are brought off so well that you would not have noticed them unless I had pointed them out. This is called in the lecturing or writing trade (as well as in the dressmaking business) "padding the subject"—which is, in our case, conducting. And all you people who have read books before kindly notice that the transition back to my topic is being done with all the finesse which Beethoven used in the transition themes of his last nine symphonies, all of which call for conductors.

It is almost time for the warning bell, so those of you who are still wide-awake may want to ask a series of questions such as "Why did you write this book?"—or, in case you are just reading it in the privacy of your own home, "Why are you offering this course?" And I am glad you asked. Most writers write for fame, money, or posterity. With me it is just a case of not being able to keep anything to myself, and as a result, what we have here is not only a book, but a two-fold book (as you will notice if you try to fold it). This is what comes of having a lot of loose paper lying around, a typewriter, and absolutely no will-power.

So what we have here is a dual-purpose excursion into the art and science of the conducting craft for both the curious music lover (and some of them are pretty curious, all right!) and for the ambitiously fame-yearning music student who wants to beat his way out of the underbrush of anonymity to the pinnacle of peak-high glory with a baton. However, although the musically curious may look on (and they are indeed musically curious to look on, some of them), I must—in order to keep my status with the Textbook Writers Guild, direct my remarks solely to the now un-batoned student (the noviate as compared to the fully frocked). And remembering my father's admonitions *and* also his shingle, I will resort to fiction only when the parable is more truth-telling than the statistic.

Probably in the whole field of textbook writing there has never been anything quite so detailed and profound on so little-known a subject as this one, and it is our job to make it all clear in simple and obtuse language. This is the purpose of this book—making it all clear. And what we are making it all clear about is "conducting" and how to become a "conductor." I say this just in the event some of you may have bought this book still thinking that it was the required text for some other university course, like *Frenetics* or *Botulism*.

To the student, ardent devotion—yea, even fervent dedication is recommended toward this richly-rewarding material. And to the music lover, it will give an insight into these unhitherto-revealed mysteries as if John Gunther himself had written on "Inside Conductors."

Nor will this book be just a collection of muchly-told anecdotes about conductors (although come to think of it, I do know a few fresh, juicy ones that I have picked up during my long and wholesome life both on and off the podium), but instead, it is to be considered a course of training which begins at the very beginning and ends at the very end, filled with helpful hints, shortcuts, and ground rules. I only wish I had been able to read a book like this one when I first started out, that's what I wish I had been able to read a book like. But alas! I had to learn it the hard way, for there were no "do-it-yourself career kits" around when I was very young. Come to think of it, there weren't even electric lights until I was about ten. That is, not in our small—but neatly kept—mid-western town.

Well, I see our time is up, and I'm sorry so many of you had to leave before my lecture was over with. If you see any of the others, remind them that there is a special treat in store for them tomorrow. In the meanwhile, to those of you who are reading (instead of actually attending class) I can only suggest that if you will lick your thumb, you can turn the page over to more of I, I, I, or—as the Romans called it—Chapter III.

Chapter III

How to Select Your Tails

We're going to take up a bunch of things in this handy do-it-yourself beat book, and first of all we're going to take up "baton-istics." No handbook for conductors would be complete without an explanation of those mystical magical maneuverings of the wrist muscles which is so much of a Maestro's stock-in-trade. Actually, the downbeat isn't nearly as important as beating the other guy to the podium, but it is necessary to know a bunch of the standard tricks and so we'll take up four-four time first in case you ever run into it.

Four-four time is that kind of time which has four "fours" in it. There are probably other books that explain this, so let's just accept it as true and then neither one of us will have to look it up. Let's just say that there are four "fours" in four-four time and that we have to beat it. And we do this with a baton about which there'll be a chapter later on no doubt. In case you don't have a baton, use a pencil with number two lead.

Grasping either end in your right hand, bring it up to around your forehead, but not up as high as where your head comes to a point—which it obviously does if you're serious about being a conductor. Now bring it down. This is called a "down-beat" and I suggest that both of us rest for awhile as we have just learned the most important thing about conducting. Next to getting something to conduct, that is. Now, let's take that again. You do it while I count:

"Down-up — down!"

Now move it to your left in a debonair fashion—a sort of "what the hell" attitude. You have just conducted the second beat of a four-four measure. How about that for progress? Here we've been at this only about thirty seconds and you're already half way through a measure!

Once you are over to the left, there is nothing else for you to do except to bring it back over to the right as far as you can reach. This is called the "three beat" and be careful to keep the sharpened end of the baton (or pencil) away from your body, as I've seen some nasty abdominal wounds resulting from careless gesticulating on this one.

Now you have your right hand out to the right at about belt level, with the angle of your armpit being about 83 degrees in relationship to your rib cage. You sweep upward now toward your forehead again and when you reach the top, you are THERE! You have beat a measure of four-four time and you are on your way to the Met at last.

Actually there should be a chart in here showing you the various directions of the beat, but we're leaving it out because we assume you already know which way down and up is and can tell your right hand from your left. If there be any among you who are not up on this phase of the craft, mail us a self-addressed stamped envelope and you will be sent a handy little direction-finder complete with genuine arrows once used by genuine Indians. Only the arrowheads have been removed to protect the awkward.

After we have mastered four-four time (with the four "fours" in it), we should study three-four time. Three-four time is one less time than four-four (if you remember your second grade arithmetic) and so in three-four time we beat once less often than in four-four.

"But WHICH one?" you are screaming impatiently and so we will tell you.

It is the one where you would have gone left if it were four-four.

In three-four time we go down, right, and then up, and the first thing you know, out comes the Blue Danube or something equally waltzy. In faster three-four, you beat only one time to the measure but you still have to count up to three. You give a down beat in the faster three tempi (or speeds) but at the same time while you are doing it, you count "one-two-three." It's sort of like a "perpetual

You'd better wear sneakers or ground-grippers.

Don't ever buy a second-hand dress suit unless you are sure that it wasn't made originally for a magician.

—*sometimes it is good to weight them down*—.

Half-moon glasses great for peering over half-moon face to go with them.

Fat man has dickens of a time keeping them on if he sweats a lot.

Pince-nez for lean faces.

If your ears sag, don't get heavy horn-rimmed ones.

downbeat" with only enough up-beats thrown in to allow you to perpetuate your downbeats. Just make sure you don't count out loud when you do this as the lip movement confuses the players no end.

This is pretty simple stuff and very well explained. I remember when I learned it, they said to describe a pattern like a three-sided polygon or right-angled triangle and so I had to take an extra half-semester in geometry to learn what that was, even. So no wonder there were no waltzes in my repertoire for awhile.

After three-four we take up five-four which is one more than four-four. But it is harder because almost nobody knows where to put the extra beat (sometimes called the "dead-beat") in five-four time. You start out like you were conducting four-four, but somewhere in there between *two* and where *three* used to be (which is already pretty far to the right) and where *one* starts (which is way up there), you've got to put in both *four* AND *five* and still get back to where you started from.

Some conductors just sort of shrug at this point, but that isn't playing fair with the men. Other conductors will walk blocks out of their way to avoid it, but as for you, prepare yourself well. Explain exactly where you are going to put the fifth at all times; never be a secret beater. And once you have told the orchestra (or band) what you are going to do, it is then up to them to either follow you or be properly chastised with words of several syllables, some of which you already know if you have hung around poolhalls any.

I remember once I had to write a piece for a conductor that I didn't like because I felt that his attitude toward my music wasn't what you might call enthusiastically noble. But HE had to conduct it and I had already spent the commission money on luxuries like food and clothing, so I HAD to write it. Well, I figured I would fix his biscuits good by changing time signatures with every bar-line and so had three-four measures followed by six-eight and five-eight and once I even put in a seven-eight. The only trouble was that HE got sick (or said he was) and I had to conduct it. Well, I learned my lesson, all right, and here lately I have stuck altogether to plain-vanilla four-four time or have written only for healthy conductors.

A friend of mine has been trying to invent a baton that has an automatic time-changer in it. He has also been working on sight-reading and transposing glasses, and if he is successful he'll make enough money to let him afford to go back to his chosen profession which is school-teaching. Until that day, students, you'll have to either learn to beat such things as five-four time or think up reasons why you shouldn't play it.

One more helpful hint. Sometimes five-four time has a stress point which enables you to divide the measure into two segments. Now five divided by two is two-and-a-half and so sometimes you can beat two and then a couple of halves (this is called the "twitch" or "uncertain" beat) and when you have repeated this gesture you will have made it all the way through the measure. However, if you get the impression that you're being followed, it won't be the orchestra that's doing it. It is best to look at the music and see what the composer is doing at the time. If he is still alive, then you can phone him up and ask him to change it. Or you can get the hang of this three-plus-two (or vice versa) easily if you will walk along the street counting out loud: "one two three four five" and at the same time flailing away with your arm first at "one" and then "three." If anyone looks at you strangely, you can always pass it off as a charley-horse or say that you were on your way to the psychiatrist anyway.

Six-eight time has two problems. Fast six-eight gets two beats to the measure and slow six-eight gets all six. In slow six-eight, you do a downbeat and then a second beat (which is about halfway in between what used to be your second beat in four-four time) and then you move on over to the left for three (where two used to be). Four is over there to your right, but don't go too far as you will run out of arm before you reach five (which is where three was in four-four and two was in three-four). Where that same spot is in five-four is optional as you damned well know if you've been practicing it.

Six (we're still talking about the same thing, aren't we) is on the way up toward your head again at the apex of the pinnacle, as it were. The whole process of beating slow-moving six-eight time is like trying to move your hand through a batch of cold molasses with a viscosity of about ten, except you don't get any on you generally.

You have to learn this one, though, because there is a lot of six-eight time around that is just aching to be beat.

I could go on and on about the other kinds of times like six-four and three-eight, but I figure you'll bone up on these yourself (if you're really serious) and will learn to adapt yourself to any occasion, come what may (even if you're like the others). Unfortunately there is no 5½ time, but there really is a neat Symphony by that name which both its publisher and its composer would appreciate your playing from time to time. We think it only "meet and just so to do" (as they say in church).

So far we have been talking about only your right hand, but if you will count them you will notice that you have two. The other hand is called the left hand and is not used for counting the numbers with at all, but it is used for "expression." There are two things you can do with this hand that are most effective, and we will take these up first.

One is called (a) the palm-up gesture, and the other (b) is called the palm-down gesture. As far as I know there is no palm-sideways gesture except maybe in the related art of karate. When you slowly bring the palm upward (with the palm itself in the "a" or palm-upward position), the orchestra will increase its volume, supposedly, and when you reverse this procedure, they will hush up some. And if you roll your fingers toward your wrist tightly, you can make what is called the "fist" and this will produce a hell of a racket, especially if you have gradually moved your left hand palm upward (in a sort of supplicating fashion) and climax the whole gesture with the fist. It is about the only place in the world where you can shake your fist at somebody and get cymbal crashes instead of an immediate brawl.

A little practice with the left hand (and it is *so* true in conducting that the left hand is NEVER to let the right hand know what it has been doing), and you can produce magnificent effects from your group, especially if they are *watching* you and happen to want to.

This left-handed lecture has now prepared us for some good basic information called (a) holds, (b) cutoffs, and (c) upbeats.

Sometimes "holds" are called by their right name "fermatas" (an Italian word meaning "holds") and sometimes they are called "birds eyes" as they do look all for the world like a bird with only one eye except for the fact that most birds don't have eyebrows. We will take up the fermata first.

There are several ways to rehearse a passage with a fermata in it. One is to get right up to it and cut the group off and bawl somebody out over some imagined grievance or other, and then start up again by saying:

"Let's begin right AFTER the fermata."

This is one of the safest ways of doing it; however, it is risky to keep on doing because it doesn't look too neat at a concert. Another way is to face squarely up to it and explain to the group exactly what you are going to do (while at the same time figuring out loud what *it is,* really, that you are going to do). It is always good to have a new member in your orchestra so you can pretend that this whole bit is for his benefit and so *please* pay attention, even though *he* knows that *you* know that *he* knows and *they* know that *he* knows that *you* know *he* knows it is mainly for *you.* Don't let that bother you, though. There just might be a right way to do this and if you can figure it out by this approach, don't hesitate. Many a man has gotten into Grove's Dictionary on less.

Or you can always take it out. Conductors do have that option, you know—no matter what composers think. You can begin this way:

"I've always felt that Mozart erred in placing the fermata here and I'm inclined to agree with Vertschlatz in his book on the *Sublimated Meanings in the Music of Mozart,* chapter two verse five, that his use of the fermata was often compulsive. Therefore, I want us to try it *without* the fermata and see how we like it and then we'll take a vote on it." So you do, but the trick is not to take a vote on it. If you get it out, LEAVE it out! And all of the newer guys in the orchestra or band will debate the whole thing later and decide that either *you're* smarter than they think you are (but they don't *think* so) or else you think *they're* dumber than *they* think they are which *they* know *they're* not. But not matter what they think, at least you've gotten rid of the fermata.

Sometimes a composer will write music that is very fast and loud and then have it stop suddenly without any warning. This is a dirty trick on both conductors and audiences, for in the case of the latter, someone is always getting caught talking out-loud to a neighbor and is embarrassed to be heard hollering into the silence that follows such a "cut-off" by the orchestra. And in the case of the conductor, it means HE has to be right there at the exact time it's supposed to happen and if he misses it one way or the other (give or take a measure or so), he looks bad. That is, unless he knows a few of the solutions to such problems.

These cut-offs are all a matter of timing and you really look great when you do it right. I feel it would be worth our time to practice up on this, because it will always cause the audience to look up and watch you and nudge each other and say: "Why they really *do* follow him, don't they?" Some of the more erudite will immediately start comparing your own cut-offs to those of John Phillip Sousa or Lawrence Welk.

You will notice that this seems to occur when there are either one or both of the following marks in the music (part of the directions, as it were): the cut-off and the GP. The GP means "grand pause" and musicians love it because it is their nature to want to "not play" every time they get a chance. They like *not* playing better than playing most of the time if the pay is the same. The best part you can write for a player is one with lots of measures rest in it, or better still, one marked "Tacet" (meaning he's silent altogether), will send him into spasms of delight. So he looks forward to Grand Pauses because he gets to rest, and so you can generally count on your players to stop, regardless of what you do. We are suggesting, however, that you do it *with them* and not go on waving your arms frantically because *they* will then know for sure that *you* and so forth. So study up on it, for it is really not only a challenge, but it's great fun to come out even with them.

The sign which indicates a cut-off is a couple of lines that look a little like two chopsticks lying side by side or like very tall quotation marks that tilt a little to the right. Both the GP or the cut-off can get you into real trouble until you get the knack of it, but they're actually fun in rehearsal, because some player is bound to slop over once in awhile and then it gives you a real chance to stand up on the podium looking hurt (while also looking for the place yourself at the same time). So when you hear them all stop playing, stop beating at once. And you do this with a gesture that resembles a kid trying to shake a wad of bubble gum off his fingers. Do this firmly and with an animated motion and then stand perfectly still.

If they are still playing, then you've got a chance to start in again with tiny beats and you can watch them like a hawk. Then when they do stop, you can repeat this gesture. With a little practice you can do it almost every time. Another form of stopping them is a sudden circular motion with both arms in toward yourself while bending forward slightly. This looks somewhat like your belt has just broken while you are wearing a loose pair of pants and you can check this by practicing it in front of a mirror with a broken belt and a loose pair of pants if you like. I can't caution you too much, however, to watch the sharp end of the baton during this action. A friend of mine got careless one day and dagged himself in the spleen so deep that even the Mayo Brothers ran out of thread while stitching him up.

Once they have stopped, you have to get them started again (the orchestra, not the Mayo Brothers), and this is always awkward if the cut-off is in the middle of the measure. It is best in this case to give a long swooping sort of arm motion like you were throwing to first base from left field, and then get back to beating again. This automatically puts the responsibility on the players themselves to get it right. The more of this sort of thing you work out, the better off you are because you can always stop them and say: "Well, I can't play it for you, too!" This line is spoken as you look sadly at the baton wishing that it could do it so you wouldn't have to have THEM around. A very good stance while doing this is to scratch at your ear like the whole thing put you in actual physical pain. There is always danger of ear infection later if you scratch too hard, but this is a calculated risk and well worth it if you accomplish your goal. Your greatest asset is a quiet shrug and a mournful look at your baton with an unspoken admission written over your sorrowful fact that *they* just aren't up to it!

Another point in our baton technique is called the "preparatory" beat. Somewhere along the way there seems to have grown up a gentlemen's agreement between players and conductors that you (the conductor) have to give them at least a hint of how fast you are going to beat the music. This is called the "up-beat" (and since the slogan of the Musician's Union as well as the Boy Scouts is "be prepared"), you are required to put in exactly one beat before the music actually begins. If a piece starts on the downbeat (toward the floor) then you give your upbeat before giving your downbeat. If the piece begins on an upbeat already, you still have to do it although in most cases it becomes pretty vague. Some very kind conductors will say to their men:

"I will give you one for nothing."

If *they* said that to him and didn't use the right inflection, they'd get fired. What he means is that he will give them their choice of several beats and when they all see one that looks good, then they can come in. This way he puts the responsibility on them again and is blameless for any errors. And one thing for sure, you can't have all those bows in an orchestra and not expect errors. As a matter of fact, this procedure often provides additional opportunities for him to stop the orchestra (especially if some player has just started to play too soon) and stamp his feet and give out with a few choice remarks about their ancestry, eyesight, and inexcusable ineptitudes.

Among other things we have to learn about is how to end a piece. This is tricky, but you'll get so you can end up with them almost every time because composers (bless their little old insecure economic conditions) generally set it up so that it's impossible to fail. This is nice, but we had better learn a gesture for it in case something slips up. Hold both hands up fairly high, but not so high that you won't be able to raise them higher as the piece gets to the vicinity of the finale, and then—when you see them take their instruments down—execute the standard *fermata-cutoff* with aplomb. Most of the time, somebody in the audience always starts applauding early (to show that HE knows that the piece is about to end) and sometimes there is more than one of these jokers, each of whom is trying to get in the first clap. This can throw you, so it's better to have a friend in the audience (who can read a score) who will yell "Bravo" and you can depend on that. When the applause starts, you can whirl toward the audience and begin bowing, or, if it really isn't over yet, you can give them *such* a frown for applauding early that either way you're off the hook about helping the music stop.

There are just a couple of other phases of wisdom that fit into this chapter and they're about getting the proper tempo and "concept." We'll take up tempo first. *Tempo* is a foreign word meaning "time," and we use it to indicate how much time it takes you to play the piece that you're playing and that's the least you can do, know what piece it is you are playing. Tempo has come to mean "speed" in music and a good rule to follow is that you are not required to set a new track record on every number you conduct. Tempo is roughly divided into two general categories such as Slow and Fast—although there are half-way points such as half-slow and so forth. It is always good to learn a few foreign words to use on your players, as it adds to the general aura of your erudition. You could say, for instance:

"This is marked *Allegro giocoso pro bono publico* and while the Metronomic marking is 144, we'll read it through *Adagio con respeto* and please pay attention to the appogiaturas, nuances, and hemoglobin."

At this very moment, give a quick downbeat (catching some of them not ready) and then stop for another one of your lectures, indicating that at least *your* ancestors don't bark! Tell them that they've spoiled your "mood," and you'll soon have them scringing. By this time any tempo will feel right to them as they play with downcast eyes and deep regret that they have shattered your soul. I might say in passing here that, if you will address the entire orchestra as a whole, you can say almost anything to them. It is only when you select some individual personally that you could get hit back.

But back to the subject of tempi (two tempos make up one tempi). This word, by the way, is pretty close to "tympani" so don't make that error or they'll send you back to music school and you'll have to be a dean. A tympani is a kind of drum usually played by very fat men or bewildered looking women. Once you get it located in the orchestra, it is great to point to when it is playing, as it gives off a hell of a boom!

Getting the tempo right (or almost right) is not too difficult if you work at it, and since it relates to "concept" (which we will take up in a minute) you can't get off too far. You can't anyway because, if you don't watch out, the orchestra will set it for you anyway. Some conductors have advocated mechanical devices and one or two of them have even resorted to such things as tiny metronomes built into the handles of their batons. Then, after writing the proper speed on their shirt cuffs, they assume a stance not unlike fervent prayer while they tune in on the correct concert beat pattern. Still others have worn what seems to be hearing-aids, but which are really small transistor radios tuned into their dressing-room sending stations. Here they have planted an accomplice (usually related to them or highly-paid so they won't tell later).

This accomplice speaks into a microphone and "talks them in" (as we say in the aviation game) with remarks like "AOK now, not too fast. It's in six, so sixfivefourthreetwoone, GO!" Neither of these methods is foolproof, for metronomes built into your baton handles are liable to start clicking loudly in soft passages and your transistor just might pick up a local rock-and-roll station the very night you're trying to get the tempo-control tower to send in the right speed for Valse Triste or something equally hard.

So it is just best to start your own tempo and hope you are in the general area. The music critics may criticize you, but heck, what do you care? You can always get back at them later by saying "What does that word merchant know about tempo—he can't even get to the concert on time!" And besides (you can always add), "he has no CONCEPT of the music!"

Concept is an important factor in all of your work. It's pretty hard to define but it's easy to have a lot of. As the man with the baton, you have unalienable rights to concept and you can alibi any wrong-doing with the simple phrase: "that was my concept of it," and then you can hastily bring in the name of some famous long-dead conductor (and also unrecorded) and say: "Serrbolt always did it in three, claiming that von Raff—who studied the score with the composer personally one summer near Geselschaft—had talked it over with him and they both agreed (because of the inner voices) that it would be better in three than in seven and at just the tempo I took it."

This will put down the critics—both in and out of the orchestra —for all time, unless for some reason they happen to have inner voices of their own. It is always better not to have any live composers around unless you think there's a possibility to humiliate them publicly by discovering otherwise unnoticed mistakes (which you have carefully put in just before rehearsal so you can discover them). This will prove beyond all doubt that your ears are always in there searching for the truth. Composers, by the way, humiliate easily at readings of their music, and if you have any sense of the theater in you or are inclined to be sadistic, it might be worth the money to commission one just to have him around. It's good clean fun for both you *and* the orchestra as it is one of the few times that the orchestra is on your side.

So use this "concept" bit to the hilt. This and a lot of quotations from little-read musicologists will cover up a multitude of sins (musically speaking, that is—you'll have to think up your own excuses if you're caught trifling with the lady tympani player) and you will go far indeed. I can just hear you now as you glare angrily at the lower woodwinds:

"Well, I *could* be wrong, but in Manzonia's massive volume entitled 'From Myerbeer to Madrigals', he says . . ." and so on and so forth and so on!

But promise me one thing about all of this, will you? Remember to keep this sort of thing as classified material. It's not that we're paranoidal, but we just don't want *everybody* to know what's really going on. Now, do we?

Thus endeth the reading for this chapter, and so we shall now proceed onward to Chapter IV which we will call "From Podium to Posterity and no hard feelings!" And if you're ready, I am. So let's do it!

CHAPTER IV

As the Twig Is Bent, So Shall the Child

I noticed just now that we got all the way through that last chapter without once getting on the subject of how to select your tails, and I would apologize except that I am not a book writer by trade and therefore can't be expected to do things right the first time out. We'll discuss this briefly now, but since you'll do as you like about it anyway, I won't make up any hidebound rules for you to follow. The first thing to do is to establish a line of credit somewhere so you can buy all of these things on time. After all, your business is "time," isn't it? You can use me as a reference if you think it will do you any good, but just don't mention that I don't have my own fully paid for yet. If you're clever enough, you can talk some prominent clothier into fixing you up in exchange for program credits (like they do on all the big TV shows where sometimes the credit listings are more interesting than the programs themselves). You could always promise to print: "tails by Robert Hall" or Maestro Glott's ensemble by Sears and Roebuck, America's Favorite Mail Order Haberdashery. If this doesn't work, then try a tailor somewhere and get him to make them by hand. This way they will fit generally and that's always good when you're up in front of the public.

If you've never worn a dress suit before (and remember we all have to begin somewhere), you can practice getting the feel of it by leaving your shirt tails out for a couple or three days. It seems to me that there's always a draft when you wear tails, but it just may be the way mine are fitted. You'll need a couple of stiff-front shirts and some clip-on ties, too. Not that I discount your ability to tie a bow tie, but if you are that clever, why do you want to be a conductor? You could make a living easier ways. Buy white suspenders and never, ever use a belt as they tend to bind the midriff and stop the flow of blood through your arteries and such. I wouldn't bother buying a top hat and cape until you are more or less regularly employed, as some folks simper every time they see a cape no matter who's wearing it unless it is a bull fighter. The two vocations are similar enough as it is without provoking comment from the un-elite.

You needn't buy any new underwear unless you're the type who is liable to lose his trousers during an especially violent movement in Tschaikowsky's 1812, or Symphony No. 5&½, or some of the other hits. One conductor I used to know always wore chip-on shorts, but it didn't work out too well because he kept getting blood poisoning from rusty flanges. Of course, you'll need other clothes, too. A full-time conductor has to have morning clothes (for conducting in the afternoon) and tuxedos for going to receptions in after concerts, and some conductors even go in for berets and Ascot ties. But remember what I said about simpering and wait a bit on this sort of extracurricular adornment.

And, oh yes. Rehearsal clothes! There are generally two types of these used. The first kind is the latest style in wild abandonment and carefree, gracious living where you wouldn't mind being photographed at rehearsal and rather hope you are. The other is an old sweat shirt, a seldom-washed towel for throwing around your neck during intermission, very baggy pants, and either sneakers or ground-gripper shoes. The latter often come in handy if the podium isn't tufted with some sort of skid-proof rug or nailed down securely. It doesn't really matter much which of these two types of rehearsal costume you choose. I'll say this, though, the latter is much cheaper and you soon cultivate the reputation of being really one of the gang by exhibiting this outward carelessness toward apparel. Watch it if someone sends you an anonymous box of Duz, though, as it's time to wash the sweatshirt when this happens!

I often think that by the time a conductor gets through buying his wardrobe, he's got so much invested in his career that he can't afford to give up. And after all the Biblical adjurements about "rent-ed garments," he doesn't dare do that even if they are (if the Internal Revenue Department will excuse the expression) *deductible*. One thing for sure in this business, you just won't work if you look like a tramp. I only hope you have the figure for tails, for if you're the chunky type, no matter what you pay for your dress clothes they won't like your Brahms. Be svelte, if you can. And it won't be too hard at first, because if you have to spend everything you make getting out-fitted, you won't have much to spend on fattening foods anyway. Or scores!

One final warning. Don't ever buy a second hand dress suit unless you are sure that it wasn't made originally for a magician. A friend of mine lost his job that way, for while soaring magnificently into etherial bliss during the slow movement of the Shostakovitch Fifth, all hell broke loose and he doesn't know to this day what magic action he threw out of kilter. But suddenly pigeons started flying out of his collar and full-grown rabbits and ducks suddenly appeared! This, plus miles of colored silk handkerchiefs that oozed out of his shirtsleeves and the fact that every time he cued the violins, lighted cigarettes kept coming out of the end of his baton, brought the whole house into a state of hilarity. And to climax it all, during one fierce lunge (whether at a rabbit or at an approaching fermata we'll never know), the whole back of his coat opened up and was transformed into a huge American Flag. As I say, it was his undoing, for when this happened the entire delegation from the Soviet Embassy stalked out in a huff and they are still exchanging notes about this in Wash-ington. So, you can't be too careful! My friend, by the way, is now working as a used car salesman in Sacramento and is relatively happy except when he hears music.

But let's say now that you're outfitted and you really look grand. Your next step is to get two full-length mirrors and set them up so you can see yourself from the back. You see, the audience only sees a conductor from the back, and all of a man's formerly-forward per-sonality has to be now projected from his flip-side (as we say in the record trade). If you are backward already, this will help, but if you are not, then you have to practice making your shanks and shoulder blades as appealing as you are frontwards to the musicians. In a hasty interjection, let me mention that your appeal to the average musician is not usually too high as they regard you as interfering with their own God-given right to be up there where you are. They see you only as through a glass darkly, tinted with jealous green, and they will always resent you as long as you are healthy. The only way to get their regard is to have some incurable disease (or at least say you have) which sort of holds out hope that they might someday replace you.

So conductors, by and large, don't get to face the audience much except during bows, appeals for funds, or the national anthems. We will speak of community singing at a more appropriate time, but for now my task is to show you how you can assure yourself that you cut a fine figure on the podium. In this form of practice (and for heaven's sakes, draw your blinds before you start) you disregard entirely such things as facial grimaces and how your nails look and so-called "stick" placement. The question is not whether you beat "three" correctly, but how do your elbows look while you are doing it! And what happens to your neck line and still more important, do your shirt cuffs stay in? I knew a conductor once whose shirt cuffs came on down over his fingers so often that the musicians used to say: "Look, Ma, no hands!" Really! Another thing is do your tails ride well at the waistline while you are in motion? If they don't, sometimes it is good to weight them down with a few fishing sinkers so they'll not start flapping around like long underwear on a clothes line on a brisk March day.

Okay, so you practice beating time so that you really look interesting from the back. Learn a few basic dance steps for your footwork and work on a few tricks like putting a little body-English on an upbeat. This effect often sends the left tail skittering around like a wounded penguin on a particularly slick ice floe and is very effective on evenings when you have programmed dull music. With the proper footwork (put your best foot forward, but never both at once) and making sure that your shoes are shined, especially on the back or (present company excepted) "heel" section, you are assured of podium success unless your garters come down or your collar comes unfastened. And this *is* possible, because I had the first thing happen to me and I saw the second thing happen. I'll interject my own exciting anecdote first.

I was conducting—one of my own works, naturally—I always operate on the theory that if Brahms and Beethoven didn't conduct my music, why should I conduct theirs? Turn about is fair play, I always say (or almost always). It was with the San Antonio Symphony Orchestra and I was absolutely resplendent in a brand new hand-fitted dress suit that it seemed a shame to wrinkle it with anything as plebian as music. My whole getup was newly bought except for my gaiters—notice the stylish effect the English spelling has on that word? These elderly garments had long served my needs and I thought nothing of trusting them on this evening. So I carefully attached them to my new silk dress socks and had barely gotten the music under way when, co-incidental with a deft combination of a *petite jeté* and a neat *riposte,* I felt that slithery feeling that can only be either a cobra winding itself around your ankle or a garter deserting its post in time of crisis. It was probably the silk in the hose—those garters had never tackled anything more genteel than cotton before—but anyway, there it was. If ever there was a time for a man to light a Murad, it was then! I went on, pretending it was somebody else's leg that the thing had slid down and did my usual brilliant job, handicapped though I was by not being able to move that particular appendage for the full twenty minutes. As the applause burst forth, I turned gingerly, not wanting to step on it and snap my tibia with a be-metaled strip of elastic as my Blue Cross had lapsed, and made my exit, shuffling all the way, looking all the world like an old-time minstrel show end-man as I did my darndest not to let the audience know that I was sartorially insufficient from the knee down. I learned my lesson. From that day on I've used thumb tacks. There's always a danger of septicemia, but your socks sure do stay up!

And as for the other man, his crisis was even worse than my own. His wing-tip collar slipped off its sprocket about eight bars after he had given the downbeat on the Sibelius 4th Symphony with a very high class orchestra, and that's just one thing you can't ever fix with one hand! But he made the mistake of trying to repair the damage

and at the same time, tried to keep the orchestra going. He fought
that collar all the way through the first movement and almost as soon
as he would get it buttoned down momentarily, it would let go with
a twang that could be heard in the second balcony. Not only was the
audience distracted, but the orchestra was convulsed and Sibelius lost
out all the way around. Rumor has it that this fellow hasn't worn a
collar on the podium since. He just painted his neck white and let it
go at that!

Another thing you ought to have in your equipment is a pipe. A
lot of young conductors make a mistake by buying long cigarette
holders, but this is a form of affectation that is easily recognizable and
besides, somebody is liable to take it away from you and use it as a
baton on an orchestra of his own. But a pipe, now there's a different
thing. Not that you need to smoke it, necessarily, but it's really a great
thing to have around for rapping to get attention with at meetings
and sort of casually scratching your temple with while at the same
time getting a far-away-look on your face as if you were contemplating something profound.

You remember those old advertisements that went: "I love a
man who smokes a pipe"? In these ads, the guy was smoking and was
always surrounded by a bevy of beauties, but you'll probably make
more friends by not smoking it. Especially among the beauty bevy set.
Use it to punctuate arguments with (or even discussions) or telling
stories about.

"This pipe," you can say, looking as sage as one of the Grimm
brothers, "has a deep place in my heart because it once belonged to
. . ." (and here you supply a name that will be a household word to
each and every one of them). The very fact that you've got this guy's
pipe (whoever he was) is enough right there to prove to your community that you've got something extra special. Just remember whose
pipe you said it was and don't go changing the name every time you
tell the story, otherwise they'll mark you down as a fabricator and not
believe anything you say, even about music. And be sure to boil the
pipe in milk every now and then too, for there is nothing gamier than
an old pipe in a hot room, no matter who gave it to you.

And since you've already got your double full-length mirrors, it's time to talk about another pair of glasses you'll want to acquire without which no conductor, even if he has two pipes, is quite complete. These are called eye glasses and they are for the eyes. Sometimes it is not enough for us to make a spectacle of ourselves, we have to keep in mind that the eyes are the windows to the windows of the soul. I take it for granted that you all have souls and haven't traded them off in some hasty deal with Lucifer in exchange for a seven-year contract at the local Philharmonic. If you have, there'll be the devil to pay and conducting is hellish enough without looking for more trouble later among the forked-tail set.

Get your glasses whether you need them or not, for there is nothing quite as sincere as a pair of heavy horned-rimmed glasses for a conductor unless it is a heavy foreign accent. There are multiple uses for these, not the least of which is an opportunity to stand up and polish the lenses while trying to remember how the next piece starts. Of course, horned-rimmed glasses are heavy, so if your ears have a tendency to sag a little anyway, get some other kind. Instead, try the pince-nez—but not unless your general attitude is professorial and your face is lean. A fat man has a dickens of a time keeping them on, especially if he sweats a lot. If you're afraid of this sort of disaster, maybe you'd better buy the kind that are attached to a chain that has a spring on it. Although come to think of it, many a man has had his nose lacerated when he did a body twist that put his face out of tether length. Some conductors look good in these half-moon glasses and they're really great for peering over. You should have a sort of half-moon face to go with this, however, or you may end up looking like an under-nourished mackerel.

Don't use the ones with thick lenses unless you have near-fatal myopia and a thick German accent to go with it. And of course, monocles are out entirely unless you are an Englishman and come by it naturally. Lorgnettes are also out for you they are restricted to boxholders over sixty with ample measurements and mink stoles. And don't buy anything that isn't shatterproof, either, for having an oculist picking glass fragments out of your eyeballs is pretty painful, I hear. Contact lenses are pretty expensive and so don't get those unless you have good contacts. You really can't see them anyway so your purposes of buying this equipment would be lost, unless (that is) you really need them. If you do need to wear them, for heaven's sake don't be bashful about it. A former student of mine (who graduated before this book came out) was so near-sighted that he lit what he thought was a cigarette for a board member's wife and it turned out to be her long skinny nose.

I've heard about one new optical invention that has been developed entirely for conductors (and not by that friend of mine who is trying to get rich enough to get back into the school teaching business, either). This one is coming on the market soon and is being manufactured by a prominent electronics firm to be sold for no small profit by eliminating the middle man. The lenses in these are really two tiny TV screens and the score you're conducting is projected (two pages at a time) on the inside of the lens, facing your eyes. They're supposed to be great for conducting concerts in what appears to be "from memory" method, thus eliminating the need for turning pages and licking your thumb all the way through the performance. I haven't tried these myself, as they tell me there's some risk to them. At least I've heard that the conductor who tried them out experimentally for the factory is now the only one in the business with Ubangi eyeballs. And the only way he'll ever conduct again is by Braille.

So get yourself the glasses that fit YOUR personality, and if it's tortoise-shell, for God's sake, remove the tortoise first as those things have the reputation of being terribly untidy at times.

I should take up etiquette here (like table manners and asking for second helping and things like that), but people won't notice which fork you pick up if your conversation is interesting enough. Buy a pretty good book either on etiquette or conversationing and you'll be okay, I think. Another thing a lot of conductors have are dogs, but I don't recommend them, for by and large they aren't too handy to have around a musical aggregation as they howl. I had a basset hound named Genius once who howled in the key of A-flat and he was nice to have around when the oboe player didn't show up for rehearsal, and for looking sad during Tristan. As a composer, I often get to see the sides of conductors' lives that have been closely guarded from the general public and, while I don't like to gossip, will tell one story about this one who had the Russian wolf hound.

He called me in (the conductor) to commission a piece out of me, and what he lived in couldn't be called a hovel by anybody's standards. And the first thing I noticed when I walked humbly into the room was this slavering beast with the yellow eyes standing over in the corner (the dog) and I knew we were really in for a session of negotiation. Personally he hated dogs, this conductor, and he only kept this one around for keeping composers at bay and for shearing twice a year (the dog) as he was fond of wearing mufflers which he passed off as being llama fur. He had this dog so trained that he growled furiously at any price over one hundred dollars and so that's what I got. He got hydrophobia later, however, (the conductor) when the hound heard him play his own recorded arrangement of "Trees" twenty-two times in one afternoon while leaving the poor animal tied up to a cactus plant. So, no dogs, fellows. After all, you don't really need them. You've got an orchestra on leash.

Well, I guess that about does it for your personal equipment except for the baton, and here I want you to pay close attention even if it means stopping your curtain-call bow practice for a few minutes. I did remind you to get a long-playing record of applause for this, didn't I?

The baton MUST be selected carefully to fit YOUR hand and you must never, no never ever let anybody else use it. This is not from fear of getting germs or not getting it back, but unless their palm perspiration has the same chemical qualities as your own, they can warp the whole thing out of balance and then where are you? Loan them your toothbrush, if you must, but never your baton because it is the TOOL of your trade. Some conductors I have heard of get a grip on a satisfactory one and just leave it there. It's a little awkward for getting your shirt on, but they just don't want to take any chances of spoiling that perfect sense of micromatic balance that a perfect baton must have to do a first rate job. And with you, genius grade, it is even more important.

And don't ever consider conducting barehanded, either. That had its fad for awhile during the depression when times were bad, but modern technology and the American Way of Individual Enterprise has now made these things available to one and all, regardless of race, creed, or color.

Select the wood carefully, preferably a non-splintering kind as there is nothing more painful than a palmful of festering sores. Don't choose a wood that's too heavy, like teakwood. That stuff is great for carving little elephants out of, but one full rehearsal with one of those dead-weight clubs and you would be muscle-bound for months.

Get one that is flexible enough to whistle when you slash it through the air, if you like. But if you do, try to select several that will at least whistle in the key you are playing in. One rule of thumb is that, if you're tall, get a big, long baton. But if you're short, get one about the length of a short knitting needle. This small size will really make the musicians have to focus to see where your beat is.

Some conductors conduct barehanded because they're afraid they'll drop their batons, but a little Elmer's glue or a rawhide thong will relieve that trauma. Don't ever use one of those metal telescopic sticks, for they have the habit of slipping their joints and the whole effect will be like beating four-four time with a thin armadillo.

I would like to suggest that you go to a palm reader and check your exact size—and while you are there, she can see whether your life line is long enough to warrant the investment. Go to a good cabinet maker and order one with a cork tip (or at least a filter) as there is a certain amount of nourishment in this in case times get bad. When you have selected one that is balanced perfectly and whistles in the right key, you're ready. Oh, one last thing. Make sure they break easily. Baton breaking at rehearsals is a sure sign to the orchestra that you're upset about something. But if you have to stand there and struggle around trying to break it, the whole effect is completely lost.

And now, students, if you have followed all my advice so far, I'll let you pick out your boutonniere by yourself. Just don't be gaudy about it, and for heaven's sake, get an allergy test before you start buying one made out of cornflowers or goldenrod. As for me, I never use them as I sneeze easily and never on beat. Remember that they are worn on the left (near the violins), and buy several as they are great for throwing graciously to the audience (in lieu of white kid gloves) during the applause.

So now that we've got you dressed (you'll have to get your valet to help you next time) let's move on to a new chapter on platform posture. And we call it: "Divers truths about little knowne and hitherto unpublished secrets about music revealed here for ye firste tyme."

Shall we *avanti?*

CHAPTER V

Mounting the Podium or Taxidermy Made Easy

Here we are again at the beginning of a new chapter and it is called Chapter Five. This is an important chapter because it relates to what happens on that little dais which musicologists, in the fullness of their wisdom, have nicknamed the "Podium." Actually if we were to look into the derivation of that word, we might get a few rude surprises, so we won't unsettle anybody by telling you exactly what it means. A defrocked music history teacher once hinted darkly to me that it has nothing to do with the feet, otherwise it would have been called "pedium." I know better, though, because it is quite a feat to get up there. I personally believe, after seeing some of the brethren operate, that the word is derived from the same one that produced "poltergeists" and you know what they are. In a recent frenzy of research I made by consulting our old friend Webster, I thought to go at it scientifically and so broke the word down into its components, the first of which is "pod." Webster (or one of his ghost writers) said of this: *"Pod: A number of animals gathered together, a school, as of seals or whales: of birds, a flock."* Well, I knew I was on the right track, at least, and the last half of the word 'ium" is like that last part of the word "auditor-ium" which is a place people go to hear things. Now mind you, it is Webster who is making the comparison, so don't blame me if you put two and two together like I did and figure that a *podium* is a gathering place for a flock of something like in a school.

I myself, without benefit of dictionary-writing training, have contrived a definition which we shall use for this course and which you may now hand down from generation unto generation as official. A *podium* is a small platform on a stage, upon which may stand (but not always) a conductor (or leader) with a musical aggregation (of some sort or another, including sometimes singers or their equivalent in effort), whose principal effect is to elevate him (or to raise up as in "scaffold") above the others." Some musical researchers claim that this platform was once called "elevatorium" by the early Romans and from this came the word "pedestal" which is a hunk of something you set a statue on.

I always think it is nice to know things like this, but it is better to know that there *are* such things and that it is our job to get on one with a musical aggregation somewhere in the vicinity so that we may use it (and them) for our very own. And because it is so important that we know what we are up there for once we get up there, we'll go back to our double fullview mirrors and resume that all-important practice that, while it doesn't seem to have anything to do with music, looks like it does. And who are we not to take advantage of the multitude's somewhat inadequate knowledge of the truth? So we will deem it all to be very necessary and I will give you two sets of exercises which you should practice, particularly to music if you have any around. You might even use stereo just to get used to having music come out at you from all directions. The first part of our lesson is called "The Profile" and the second part pertains to "Posture" with certain attentions toward the "Leap."

We have—as you can remember from looking at pictures on "Wanted" posters at post offices—two sides of our faces. Actually we have four, but we will eliminate the face-forward pose as we don't use it much except for looking over our shoulder disgustedly at late comers who arrive wearing heels with tap plates, and at mothers with crying babies. If you want to, you can practice this look which is sort of half-way between a leer and like you just smelled a polecat in the smokehouse. Come to think of it, if you are serious about being a conductor, you won't have to practice at all. You probably already have it!

Anyway, this leaves the other sides which are called (a recent medical doctor told me that my command of anatomical terms was nothing short of uncanny) (a) the back of the head, (b) the left side of the face, and (c) the other one. Many times also the top of the head is used, but this is not effective unless it is (a) totally bald—in which case it can be tinted with small sequins to give a dazzling effect under certain lighting conditions—or, (b) covered with a massive mane-like swatch of hair that becomes increasingly unmanageable with each shake of the head. If you *are* bald, don't ever wear a wig (sometimes called a "rug") as there is nothing more devastating to a career than to have your toupee tumble down over your eyes while you are conducting an especially dynamic performance of the Overture to the Barber of Seville.

But to get back to profiles. There is little that can be done with the back of the head and so we'll just use it as a pivot point for our right and left profile views. Practice swinging on a 90-degree angle with the vortex of the orbit balanced delicately with the nose tilted slightly upward—the "polecat in the smokehouse" stance will do fine here, also.

To your left will be the violins if it's an orchestra. God knows what it will be if it's a band! The violins are the ones they tuck under their chins and play with a bow. When you turn your head toward them, shake it a little to let your hair quiver a bit if it's nice and long, or to let your sequins glisten if you're bald. Don't turn your body, though, as this is another gesture. Practice turning to the right, also, but not too quickly as you can get damned dizzy and start wobbling around like a punch-drunk pug if you're not careful. When you turn to the right, you will generally see the *"celli,"* and although they *look* like violins, are seldom if ever tucked under the chin to be played. Any of *this* you see, you had better report to the union at once!

Step two in profiling is to turn the upper part of your body at the same time you turn your head. Make sure they both go the same direction or that popping noise you hear won't be percussion, and you'll end up with your neck in a sling. When you turn to the violins (they're under the chin), reach your left hand up to your chest and gracefully bend your fingers against your body and wiggle them. This looks like you are helping them produce their vibrato and has a very

No dogs, now fellows!

Some conductors get a good grip on a baton and hang on!

sexy effect on the dowagers in the audience. Don't press too hard, however, especially if you are ticklish. And make sure you have washed at least your left hand as there is no point getting your white vest dirty. And, oh yes! Wait until you are sure the violins are playing before you do this. Getting out of this position is easy if you plan it well and wait until the cymbals crash. At that moment, throw your left hand into the air as if you were tired of having it around. It looks really great from the audience if your dress shirt cuffs are not loose. This same gesture is effective toward the right, but never exaggerate it toward the *celli,* as remember they hold them between their knees and there might be a few people in the audience that would misunderstand the whole effort.

Step three in profiling is the complete turn. When you notice the violins are going strong, turn around and pretend to be one of the Three Musketeers and, using your baton as a rapier, slash and swirl like you were rescuing the princess from the dragons. Caution: if they start to fight back, turn quickly toward the trombones. They're further away. A few hours of practice of this sort of thing in front of the mirror will give you an edge on the more untutored fellows who just stand up there beating time. And it's not really a waste of effort even if you don't make it as a conductor. You can always go into ballet!

There are certain advantages in learning all there is to know about music (I have always said), but just because you do is no guarantee for success. You can study symphony scores until your brains curdle, but unless you know your way around that little magic box called the podium, you might as well take up something like prawn seining or mat weaving. You also must know something about the other arts like statue making and oil painting. And we'll take some of it up right now so you can see how it relates to conducting— which is what we've been talking about, in case some of you have been inattentive.

Not that we insist that you start painting pictures or sculpting. It's only that we want you to look them over carefully and then select some of the best poses to incorporate into your work. Take the one called "The End of the Trail" by someone or other. This is the one where there is this Indian and his Pony and they're both really beat. There's a certain pathetic quality about all this that fairly droops and you can use that same slack muscle posture to get all sorts of sympathy and empathy from the audience when you finish up a piece, looking too tired to even sweat. Study some of the El Greco paintings, too. Those fellows look positively de-veined and you can use this well in fund raising. You can stay away from the Dutch school entirely except for banquet speeches when you want to exude a feeling of "hail fellow, well fed." It's a shame they don't use banjos or guitars in symphonies much, because there are several nice paintings with lutes and lyres that would be great to use during the pizzacato. Look this word up later, fellows, because it's something the strings do and you should know what they are doing when they are doing it.

There's a great painting you could emulate as the perfect pose to take while latecomers are tromping in. It's "George Washington Crossing the Delaware" and if you've got a classic brow, this one is for you. "Whistler's Mother" and "September Morn" are both out, however, and stay away from things like "The Angelus" or "The Gleaners" of Millet because they radiate humility and the less of this you let creep into your work, the further you'll go. The famed "Mona Lisa" (the picture which Hollywood made into a story) is a good one for you if you can get that vague grin down pat. It's wonderful to use while getting compliments, indicating self-assured modesty and that you really don't think they should pay you such a tribute even if it is true and muchly deserved. Blend this in with a "who, me" look (or if you are educated, "whom, I") and look down at the floor occasionally, if not in modesty, you can at least check on whether any of your garters have come down.

This "Mona Lisa" look is also pretty good to wear whenever you hear something nice about another conductor if you can remember to hum a couple of choruses from Stainer's "Crucifixion" while looking like Caesar saying "Et tu, Bruté." I know of one conductor who combined the Mona Lisa routine with "The Thinker" and while he isn't working much anymore on the podium, he has made a fortune modeling for Mad Magazine.

Statues are really better to study than pictures because they go all

*You can practice a look which is half-way in-between a
leer and like you just smelled a polecat . . .*

Whatever you do, stand tall in the saddle.

the way around and a painting generally has nothing on the back of it but the price. You can see exactly how you would look from the vantage point of the audience, and I personally advocate this type of study more than pictures. Take Rodin's "The Thinker." While you can't actually use it much during a concert (he's sitting down, remember?) it's really great for rehearsal breaks or back in your dressing room following concerts. This pose, plus some foggy contact lenses, will really make you seem like it's hard to return to the mundane reality of mundane reality. People will think you're really deep in profound thought and say "He's the biggest thinker I've ever seen, bar none."

Avoid such statues as "Venus de Milo" as you aren't built for it and you need something with arms on it. And (like that warning I gave you about loose cuffs) it could result in the orchestra snickering among themselves and using that "Look, Ma, no hands!" wheeze again. Never go out of your way to look ridiculous in the eyes of the players. They don't need any help in this matter.

There's a great one called "The Gladiator" if you have the muscles for it and can also scowl. But a better one is "The Discus Thrower." That's really a great one! Go around to the museums and you'll not only pick up some ideas, but you'll probably run into some of your Symphony Board members as they are generally a part of that crowd, too. Look them over (the statues, I mean) and make your selection and then rush home to practice so that you'll really look classical from behind.

But whatever you do on the podium, stand tall in the saddle. You are (and here I may mix my metaphors a bit, but this whole idea is excitingly provocative), you are sitting astride a podium Pegasus with the orchestra representing the front part of it and you represent the rest. So never once forget that it is your end that symbolizes conductors to all musicians, and so—like Apollo—drive your fiery chariot across the sky with the baton in your hand transformed into the thunderbolts of Zeus, so that all can see that the Winged Victory is yours! All of this sounds a little like a half-time pep talk by a losing football coach, but I feel strongly about this sort of thing and wanted to buck up your spirits a little before we go into the final phase of your lesson on "podiatrics" (a scientific term for it that I have just coined). But before we do this, we will have a short intermission and you can gather around me informally (the smoking lamp is lit) and we'll chat a few moments about off-stage conduct which may or may not, as the case may be, be of help to you later on.

Try to remember that even when you are off the podium physically, symbolically you are still up there. So act like it. While not being exactly aloof, maintain a position of lesser immortality at least while you are walking around on earth. At cocktail parties, for example, develop a stance not unlike that of a classical marble statue of the period of Pericles. Just remember the difference between being marble and being stoned and never look like that immortal line "The stag at eve had drunk his fill." We want you to have that faraway look in your eyes but not glassy to the point of ossification. Avoid the Napoleonic pose, instead adopt a sort of kingly attitude as you dispense your conversational larghesse. Too many martinis, though, and you can make larghesse out of yourself. Be complimentary in a gracious sort of way toward the ladies, but outright flattery will have them referring to you as the Abominable Snowman. Read a book on polite phrase making and every once in a while do something thoughtful like lighting somebody's cigarette and saying how nice their wallpaper is.

Don't wear fancy clothes like togas or turbans just to attract attention. You attract attention just because you are *you* and you will never be lonely as crowds will gravitate to you and ask your opinions and tell you about their gifted nephews and neices. You can wear medals, but even here don't be too ostentatious about it. A cluster or so at a time is sufficient and often a brilliant conversation piece if you are a fast thinker. When you are asked for your autograph, respond with faint modesty as if it were you, instead of they, being honored. When adulated, pretend that—while you don't really like it, it hasn't turned your head any and you are that same simple boy basically that you were back in the manger. "You feel sometimes" you tell the chic girl reporter from the Gazette after a particularly crushing onslaught of autograph seekers, "like a lion that has just been thrown to the Christians" and she will think it so cute that you've mixed up the metaphor so delightfully that she'll write all of your sayings in the paper, establishing you as a sort of reincarnated George Bernard Shaw or Oscar Wilde.

At all times, maintain a proper decorum and try to stay out of the gossip columns, avoiding any hint of scandal or wrong-doing. If this were not a family type book, I could give you some sound advice on boudoir-bundling that would curl your hair, but we won't have time for that anyway as I have just heard the warning bell and it is time to fasten our seat belts for the last part of this lesson. For those of you who are interested, however, please remain after class.

Part II of Platform Postures has to do with footwork. Prerequisites for this are two semesters with Arthur Murray and a good chiropodist. This part is pretty hard to learn and I wouldn't advocate it at all if I didn't think you were pretty agile already. If you're the pudgy type that has to wear a corset with whale bone stays, this kind of stuff can be dangerous. Many a conductor has been hospitalized indefinitely as a result of a lung puncture brought on by gazelle-like leaps and a sharp girdle brace. But let's say you are untummied and have all sorts of biceps measurements. It would be great if you had played leap frog a lot in your youth or had at least run the high hurdles in high school. But lacking that you probably have done some fly casting and this is a marvelous training for triangle beats and choral conducting.

Leaping should be restricted to a limited type of music such as (a) extremely loud beginnings, (b) music that suddenly bursts forth from very soft to fast and loud, and (c) endings which you are sure of. Make sure also that the podium has been firmly clamped to the floor, as a skidding podium is no place for a leaper. And don't place it too near the edge of the stage, either, unless you have a railing to keep you from doing a back flip into the pit below. Since only a few members of the audience actually know that noisy climaxes with cymbals and bass drums and tympani poundings would happen even if you weren't there, it is best to keep this information classified by timing all of your actions to the split second.

We'll begin our study of these procedures with the "heels up and arms high" step, the easiest of these pre-orbital command gestures.

Some conductors advocate elevated heels that have hydraulic controls and which can either be pre-set (on a time basis) or which have electronic ears that react to decibels much as an electric eyebeam works to open a supermarket door. These mechanical devices are frowned on as being unreliable, however, and there is nothing more embarrassing than being unexpectedly elevated six or eight inches during a quiet passage in Mozart. Or in case of failure of components, to be raised up on one set of toes while being caught flat-footed on the other. And it really isn't necessary, for most of us can raise up on our toes at least once or twice during the evening without causing a coronary. Don't go so far as walking on your toes like a ballerina, though, because it is hell on the tendons and, like capes and berets, may cause simpering among the audience that would give rise to conjecture.

Another dramatic move (step II we will call it for want of a better name) can be co-ordinated with your "Discus Thrower" stance and in this one you take a giant step upward with one foot while throwing your clenched fist high in the air with that "Seig Heil" attitude. Not only is this dramatic, but in case your skivvies have crawled up on you, it also takes care of that problem. Caution: Don't do this during music that has a slow tempo or you'll look like a man trying to wade out of quicksand.

The "lunge-forward-small-leap" is good if accompanied by a 180-degree swathe with the baton from left to right. This often has a frightening effect on the musicians, however, as they are afraid you might lose your grip on the baton and impale one or more of them. They have a tendency to duck down behind their music stands and some of them may even run up a little white handkerchief on a violin bow, indicating surrender, if you use this too often. If you *do* happen to catch one of them in the trajectory of your flying baton, however, it is only a manslaughter charge in most states. Even when justified.

In chromatic passages that end up with a big cymbal crash, you can flex your leg muscles and really give a jump. Cymbal players will hate you because it takes the spotlight away from them. Some of these days one of those fellows is going to slice himself right in two with one of those things and I hope I'm there to see it as they do make the

—it is only a manslaughter charge in most states.

The 180-degree swath with the baton may have frightening effect on you players—.

damndest noise. I personally have very sensitive ear drums and one or two bangs an evening with a heavy-handed cymbal clanker does to my ears what a flashlight bulb does to my eyes except it is more embarrassing for your ears to be twitching out of rhythm with the music. So when you see them getting set to wham one, just jump a little higher than he can hold the cymbals. It is the only way you have to get even with him for giving you the ear ache. Practice this leap carefully—it looks all the world like a man falling out of a hammock except in reverse. It *IS* dangerous, however, but your audience will love you for executing it correctly, especially if there's no net.

A little native ingenuity and a few old Tarzan pictures will allow you to develop unlimited podium techniques. Don't jump too far up if you get nose bleed easily at high altitudes, as many members of the audience are apt to swoon at the sight of blood. At best this sort of podiumistics is a calculated risk to life and limb on your part, but well worth it. Some of our better conductors these days are even being considered for the Olympics, although there's a nasty rumor going the rounds that at least one of them is using a trampoline to get some of his better effects. And this just isn't cricket, not rating the Good Housekeeping Seal of Approval, Music Division.

Just always remember one thing, fellows! If they ever repeal the law of gravity while you're on your way up, you may be the first man in orbit without benefit of space control!

CHAPTER 5½

The Three B's Plus One

There is an ancient yarn which almost always gets a laugh that I shall use here, not only to illustrate a point, but to try to get a laugh. The point it illustrates is "A little knowledge is a dangerous thing," so if you want to stay out of danger, either have a lot of it or none at all. The story is about this lady who came up to a conductor who was in charge of a salon group in a hotel. Or was it a hotel group in a saloon? I never can remember. Anyway, she said to him:

"Maestro, do you do request numbers?"

He smiled graciously, revealing a full set of capped teeth. He was no fool, for there is nothing so important for smiling with on TV than capped teeth.

"Why yes, madam. What would you like to hear?"

"I would like for you to play Handel's Largo," she gushed.

"But madam," he protested, "we just this minute finished playing it!"

"Oh," she said sadly, "I wish I had known. It's my favorite number."

This story graphically illustrates our dual problem in the relationship of the audience to the conductor and vice versa and I frankly don't know which vice is versa. But since we are leading you gently up to the real meat and potatoes of this chapter "How to get a job" (that 4th B in music these days is "budget") please pay close attention for your very future may well hang on the wisdom of these words. There will be a written test at the end of the period, so pay attention and it wouldn't hurt you to hearken a little bit too.

We were going to give you some helpful hints in selecting your repertoire in this chapter (or what to conduct until automation comes), but when we realized that this could be a big waste of time for you unless you actually are employed, we are postponing this study until you have signed your name on the dotted line of a break-proof contract. Then, and then only are you a real conductor and not until, no matter what they say in music school. Anyway, you can always get down to the music end of this business when you are working regularly.

Let us say that you have been asked to come to a fine midwestern city with schools and churches and miles of paved streets and its own sewage disposal plant. And you are to meet with the Board of Directors of the local Symphony Orchestra which is made up of leading citizens, except for one union representative that hasn't played a note since the William Jennings Bryan rally in nineteen-ought-twelve. While we're spinning this fantasy, we might also indicate that this same set-up works for band directors being interviewed by school boards, except for their insistence in knowing about your college degrees and whether or not you know how to drive a school bus.

On the board is an attorney, a banker (who holds the mortgage on the local concert hall), three bediamonded dowagers of indefinite ages whose best qualifications for being there are that they still have money left despite the federal government, a local minister, the mayor, and the public school music supervisor who is not only an ancient spinster, but somewhat tone-deaf besides. And you have been called in for an interview because (a) you are secretly related to one or more of them, (b) you have just won some sort of prize conducting in Moscow, or (c) they are scraping the bottom of the barrel. Normally when there is an opening in a symphony, a huge tent city mushrooms at the edge of town with conductors pouring in like it was the opening of the Oklahoma Territory or the Yukon Gold Rush. But you aren't one of these. You are different. You are (somehow) in the very room with the people who can put you on the podium. You know what you want (which is a job) and they know what they want—which is not necessarily you unless you convince them of this.

What they want, first of all, is a young man (but not too young) who can "grow" with the orchestra and the community. They want some one who speaks well and is willing to serve on every public spirited committee in town, to attend every social function, to make talks to clubs, banquets, teas, and PTA meetings. They want him to be extra man at dinner parties, write articles for magazines, dream up public relations gimmicks, give advice on what kind of piano they should buy for the den, and also conduct the orchestra—looking like a combination of all of the world's greatest conductors, living and dead. If possible, they would like to have you single (although virilely so—but not too much as we might have a scandal like you-know-who-over-in-you-know-where) or, if married have a nice little mousey-type wife who doesn't say anything much but just nods her head now and then. And, oh yes, you should be a world-shaking authority on music, but that phase of your ability will be judged by a local music critic whose qualifications for holding his post are based on the fact that he once took fife lessons and wrote his Masters' thesis on "How Father Became a Successful Newspaper Publisher."

Let's take up the "well-traveled" part first. You can really impress them by rushing into the room all out of breath, putting your airline-bestickered briefcase down, and saying: "I hope I'm not late. There was trouble with the jet at Orly." This will immediately provoke a question about Paris from one of the dowagers who was in France shortly before World War I, and you can say: "Ah, Paris . . ." at the same time kissing your finger tips and rolling your eyes around suggestively. This really tittilates the girls and you will get a giggle (and votes) out of them almost every time. This phrase "Ah . . . . .!" when applied to a foreign city (you can supply your own cities after a brief glance at Rand McNally's. In the meantime we suggest Bombay, Rome, Bangkok, Moscow, London, and Johnson City) really will come in hand for it immediately indicates to them that YOU know the city and this prevents questioning from people who have just gone through there on the bus or studied it in seventh grade geography.

As to languages, I would advocate getting a few sets of those recorded language-study courses and memorize a few phrases in several different tongues. I studied this way myself, and while I really can't talk too well to real people in their native lingo, I'm really great whenever I meet up with a 33⅓ LP who wants to know where the train station is or how is my aunt. Be sure to learn things like "What?" and "Would you mind repeating that again, *Silver plate?*" and "Thank you." And try to memorize a few expressions like "It is as you say, sir or madam, as the case may be" as more than three or four words in any foreign language sounds to the average listener like you grew up there.

I once learned a phrase which goes: *"Faro lo stesso con un pezzo di gesso, nella lavagna,"* which sounds all the world like a profound quotation from Dante, and all it means is "Do the same thing with a piece of chalk at the blackboard." I mean, it's the *way* you say it! Caution: if there happens to be one of the committee who really does speak French or Italian, indicate that you'd rather wait and have a private chat with him later over a bowl of onion soup or a mug of Chianti, adding "the others, you know . . ." With the right shrug combining pity for their ignorance and "Thank goodness, there's one cultured fellow here," you'll win a friend (and a vote). In any event, you can always say later that you've given these other languages up for Lent and now that you're *here* you think its only right that we use *their* language.

Have a brief talk ready on how you want to grow up with the community. You can bone up on this by reading the Chamber of Commerce gook and finding out some of the town's historical traditions by talking briefly with the lady at the local public library (who is probably the music supervisor's other spinster sister) and work all of this stuff into your talk. Be sure to mention names of the town's foundering fathers if you find out that any of them have descendants on the board. Tell them that *their* ideals are *your* ideals and that *you* WANT to be guided by *their* judgments entirely.

The public school supervisor will ask you right off if you mind conducting a massed choir made up of 600 eighth graders and you can tell her that you will be guided entirely by her judgment. You now have *her* vote as she has been trying to get those same kids on a platform with the symphony ever since they were in the third grade.

Notice that so far, no one has asked you anything about music except the public school music supervisor. The union representative from the local A.F. of M. will ask you for your views on labor and you can say that your grandmother once went to a spring formal with Samuel Gompers or else you can quote that passage in the Bible which says: "Render unto Caesar the things that are Caesar's." This latter, for those of my readers who may be uninformed, relates to one J. Caesar Petrillo, who for several centuries was in charge of the musician's union, the tightly-knit group controlling the fellows whom you will be conducting at when and if you get this job.

One of the dowagers may raise a ring-encrusted hand at you timidly to ask: "Tell me, Maestro, what do you play?" This is always a sort of embarrassing question because more than likely if you could really play an instrument well, you might not be out looking for a job at all. So you can suggest that you *had been* a child prodigy, but unfortunately you had contracted a severe case of pedagogy as a youth and your career was curtailed abruptly. However, in the same breath you can hint at a practiced knowledge of all the instruments except piano. People always expect conductors and composers to play piano somehow and if you admit to any knowledge of it, you'll be forever playing accompaniments for local opera aspirants or at Rotary Club sings. I once went to a PTA meeting and right out of a blue sky the Chairwoman announced that I would accompany them in the Star Spangled Banner. My own powers at the piano are limited to a few hits like "The Merry Farmer" and "Jesus Loves Me" as I could never get the hang of putting my thumb under for the stuff that has scales in it. I could get it under all right, I guess, but by the time I got it out, I had already thrown the composer's intentions into a sort of clinkerish mayhem. So I protested mildly to the lady who asked me to play our national anthem, but somehow or other I got forced into it and found myself sitting at PS 101's antiquated Beckstein and the

*I've taken to wearing bandages on my hand—not enough
to interfere with my holding a martini glass—.*

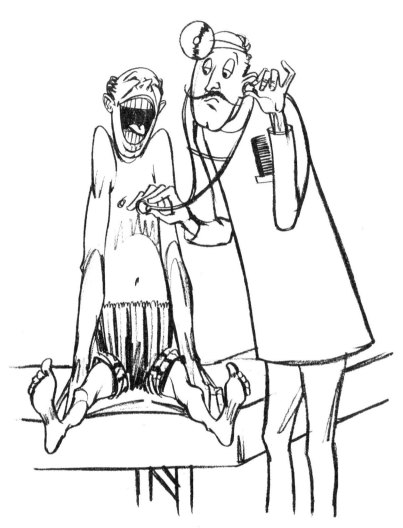

*Now being a conductor is somewhat the same status of
being a medical man—.*

catastrophy that followed (had it become generally known nationally) would have sent the stock market skittering down to a new low.

I slunk on home, pleading with them not to report me to the House Un-American Committee for subversive malpractice and went promptly to my studio where for nine consecutive days I practiced playing the Star Spangled Banner until I could play it in three keys, not just the Francis Scott Key. But do you know, in all these years since, I've never been asked even once to play it again anywhere—and it's a shame, for what I do in the part about the rocket's red glare is nothing short of sensational! So, since hostesses are always coming up to you and saying "I had my piano tuned today especially for you," deny categorically that you can play. I've even taken to wearing bandages on my hands—not enough to interfere with my holding a martini glass, but certainly enough to have a reason not to fumble around with "The Merry Farmer." This may sound a little deceitful, students, but one's musical virtue (and reputation) have to be protected at all costs.

The attorney of the Symphony Board will now clear his throat and ask a question about music. He will say: "We're not much on *modrun* music here, especially those damned Reds like Chester Kovitch and that crowd. But if you have to play it, make sure it's AMARican. That last guy we had around here was a real pinko and I told him if he ever played any of that stuff again, we'd fire him and he did and we did." This is what is known as a rhetorical question with overtones of warning. You protest immediately that you have no intention of playing this stuff which really isn't music at all, and who do those fellows think they are with their twelve tone stuff if eight tones were good enough for our founding fathers!

You may be asked about your politics, too, and you can answer them by saying "One of my ancestors was a drummer boy with George Washington at Valley Forge and was a Federalist, I believe. Either that or a Whig." Both of these parties are now out of existence and so, therefore, *safe*. But it will prove beyond a doubt that music has been running in your family since way back. But whatever your answer, just end it up with: "I plan to be guided by your judgments entirely in this matter as most of us dedicated artists have so little understanding of the machinations of political movements."

You see, all the way through you have on advantage over these people because *you* are a conductor. Now being a conductor is somewhat the same status as being a medical man, say like an obststrician or a proctologist. All over the country folks go into doctor's offices and let people they've never seen before peer in and around them, gag them with tongue depressors, take their blood pressures without so much as a "Thank you," and thump them on the back like they were testing a watermelon to see if it was ripe enough to plug. On top of that they get blood out of your finger like Dracula lived in the basement and they are forever asking you to breath deeply while listening to your innards with an ice cold stethescope. And this from strangers, mind you! No telling what they would do if you were friends. Well, it's the same way with conductors except not quite so antiseptic. If you wear the title "conductor," it is just automatically indicated that, if there is anything to know about music that you don't know, well then, you sure don't know what it could be.

So keep this attitude always aloft in your thinking and smile wisely and toy with your horned rimmed glasses if the going gets rough. It won't stay rough (at least on music) because YOU are the conductor and therefore and so on and so forth. It's on these other subjects that you have to keep your wits about you. Like organizations you belong to, for instance. Don't ever go to a meeting like this wearing emblems of fraternal orders such as Masons or Elks until you see how the land lays. If the Chairman is an Elk and has his tooth in plain sight, then—and only then—is it safe to give him the secret grip.

The minister will want to know about your religious proclivities and it is well to answer him with a couple of non-committal verses from Leviticus and like that. Or you might say that you worship at the throne of the unknown god of music, unless you know that you're in a Presbyterian community, and then add the word "predestined" in there somewhere. It isn't as if these people really care if you're a Methodist or a Lutheran, it's just that they don't

You have to watch them like a hawk!

CAUTION: Don't schedule the Mendelssohn Scotch Symphony and Handel's Water Music on the same program—.

want any unusual religions around like Zen-Episcopalianism or Nepotism. If yours is a standard brand, O.K. Or, if you look like a willing convert to the minister's flock, you've got his vote and he can fill another pew. If the town is predominately Roman, you can hint at an audience with the Pope, which, if you're the usual transient conductor looking for a job, just may have been one of the few audiences you've ever had.

The Mayor (he's the local commander of the VFW and an ardent bagpipe player in their drum and bugle corps) will want to know about your military service and you can always sigh and say that you don't like to talk about those dreadful days on Bataan. Either that or claim to have been in espionage (on *our* side) and infer (or imply) that all of that part of your life is still highly classified material. Of course, if you really were a general or something high like that, out with it. But the odds are against it. Most of the conductors I know about who were in the service barely made KP Junior Grade in some stateside camp for the unadjusted.

If you have a wife, claim that she knows nothing about music and couldn't carry a tune in a tub. This will get a laugh and also assure the dowagers that she won't try to run their musical soirees. If you don't have one, talk mysteriously about this girl in New Delhi who's a medical missionary to some remote tribe on the River Kwai estuary and until she gives it up and comes on home, you guess you'll (and here you sigh deeply) just have to wait. This will immediately get you in good with the ladies, because everyone of them has a few nieces who would make the perfect wife for a symphony conductor. Even the spinster public school music supervisor will flutter hopefully for a brief instant.

They are now almost through with you except for the banker, and he will quiz you thoroughly about your plans for balancing the budget, building the box office receipts, cutting the expenses, and your views on government spending under those bastards down in Washington who are sending this country to hell in a hand basket. Try to be humble about your knowledge of finance, but insert phrases indicating intimate friendship with the Morganthaus, Rothschilds, and the Chase Manhattans. And as to your salary, you will be guided by their good judgment. You'll have to be anyway, so it is just the thing to say. Normally a conductor's salary is fixed by multiplying the local union scale by the number of musicians in the orchestra, so don't fail to check the union price list before signing anything.

"What do you plan to pay for your season next year?" you can ask coyly, as if you really didn't care but it's one of those matters that just has to come up. When they tell you how many weeks you have to work and before they say exactly what *they* have in mind, hastily interject that you are considering offers from the London Philharmonic and the Verksmelter Vegansettblat (adding "ah, Vienna" as a teaser) and they may come up a little. Finally you have agreed and you sign a contract for a three year trial basis with twenty concerts each year for $18,000 and all you can eat at banquets and PTA potluck suppers. They will then bring up their lists of soloists (whom they have already engaged without consulting you, including two local debutantes who are related to one or more of them) and they will tell you: "Unless we have big name soloists, absolutely nobody will come to the concerts!" This isn't flattering, even if true—which it seems to be (true, that is) and they deplore the paucity of really cultured people in their town, hoping now that you're here, that things will look up.

The real reason they want the big name soloists, of course, is that they like to meet them at planes and trains and have them over after the concert for parties which will establish them even more firmly as the social lions of the town. And to this end, they've already rationed them all off and everyone is happy except the spinster who drew the Ponca City Bell Ringers instead of the robust basso from the Met that she had been hoping to show her collection of pitchpipes and tuning forks to. But, you don't really resent the fact that they've hired all of these people already even if they do get paid more than you, especially when you stop to think that you're making more than all the rest of the orchestra put together.

You sign and hands are shaken all around (yours have been shaking ever since you came in), and you are so elated about the whole thing that you agree to play the "Blue Danube" for one of the ladies who once knew Johann Strauss personally ("The younger, my dear, I never could bear the father!"). And you go back to your hotel and it's a little like the night before Christmas as visions of sugar plums dance through your head. You're IN! And all's right with the world and God is in His high heaven beaming proudly down at you.

And then it happens!

You pick up the paper the next morning to read all about yourself being the new conductor, and find instead:

SYMPHONY SEASON CANCELLED

Local Philharmonic Board

Spurns Last Union Offer

And the story goes on and on ad nauseum as your career goes down the drain and your gloom bucket runneth over.

"Oh well," you say grimly, "I can always go back to Ypsilanti and take on the beginners band again!"

And so you leave town, tails between your legs like a whipped basset, hating the world and already planning to give those kids hell next semester.

But Hark!

Maybe it didn't turn out that way at all and you got the job and everything is ahead of you, including the future. This being the case, you're lucky to have this next chapter to read which we will call "Composers, Large and Small," or "How to build your programs so you can please everybody, including the little old lady who likes Handel's *Largo.*"

Whatever *that* is.

CHAPTER VI

Composers, Large And Small...
Or, What's The Score?

If you remember, we got you a job in the last chapter and now we want you to settle down and figure out what kind of music you want to beat time at and there are as many pieces available for you to conduct as there are recordings for you to learn them by. In the olden days, conductors went scurrying around looking for new pieces to put on their programs because their audiences didn't want to hear the same things twice. And they liked good long programs, too, with two or three symphonies, a concerto or two, and maybe a smattering of overtures. None of this short program stuff for them! But this was before TV and instant everything and the current popularity of short programs makes your work a little easier because your repertoire doesn't have to be as bulky.

In the olden days, too, conductors went around to music publishers to see what they might have to suggest and some of the more daring of them even talked face to face with composers. Today the best source of information seems to be the Schwann Catalogue of LP recordings or some other good Thesaurus of Discography. This and a charge account at Sam Goody's in New York and you're on your way. This will also be a good time to point out to you that, while the musicians themselves have to keep their place only on a single line of music, you've got to use a book with everybody's part in it. Once they called this the "partitura," but now everyone goes around calling it "score."

Dr. Barry Berry, an eminent musicologist and musical anotator describes your job with a score so lucidly that I'll just crib what he said instead of thinking up something equally clever myself: "At the top," he begins, "you will find the woodwinds and things like that. Near the middle are the brasses and French Horns. Then comes the percussion, and under them, the strings." This is a very handy guide in knowing where everything is and quite well explained, I think. He also has a chapter on clefs and key signatures, but it was much too deep for me. You might like it, though, since the more you know or at least the more it seems you know, the easier it will be to remain master of the situation—at least verbally.

For every conductor who has his own orchestra, there are hundreds who don't and they will try every trick in the book to get yours away from you. Not only should you beware the Ides of March, but watch it during those other months, too! So one of the things we have to do is to play music that our board likes and then play music that our audience likes and this brings up music literature.

If all of the works for band and orchestra and chorus which have been written since the invention of notes were stacked on top of each other, we wouldn't need a rocket to get to the moon. We could walk. For composers have, to say the least, been busy (or "prolific" as it is called) for many years. The problem before us then, gentle friends, is which scores to play. This has already been partly solved for us by the fact that music (like all Gaul) is divided into three parts: (a) popular, (b) classical, and (c) unknown. Popular music doesn't count unless you want something to sneer at or to get a lot of applause with as encores. Unknown music doesn't count at all because, if it weren't unknown, then we would know it and then it wouldn't be in that category any more. The only thing it gets to do now is mildew in publishers warehouses. I have some pretty unknown music myself, come to think of it.

One of my problems was always with my titles. Take for instance "Thoughts Provoked on Becoming a Prospective Papa" which was a neat little suite of five movements that I was sure the American Obstetrical Society would take up as a theme song in their advertising, but it didn't work out that way and I'm sorry now I just didn't call it Opus 32, Number 6, in A Flat. Foreign

sounding titles always come off better on a program than those
in plain English (except in foreign countries) but how are you
going to translate "Scherzofrenia" into Dutch or Sengalese? Lots
of composers use titles like "Pastorale" and "Sonata Allegro" and
this looks a lot more dignified than things like "Bing, Bang, Bong"
or "Variations on a Kitchen Sink" (which are a couple of my lesser
unknowns). Shakespeare (or was it Bacon or Marlowe?) said:
"What's in a Name?" and then he goes on to talk about how a
rose would smell, so maybe it's not the names after all that keeps
them anonymous. I've written so much music with a western flavor
to the titles that at least half of my fans think I write my scores
astride a pinto pony with a branding iron. I had an agent once
who said "We've got to send out brochures and press releases and
pictures and flood the country with them until we make your
name a household word, like . . . like . . . Drano!" Like they say,
"What's in a name?" So much for one of my favorite unknowns,
me—and now back to music.

It is the third, or 3B classical category that we are most concerned with and one of the first things we have to do is to learn
to pronounce it. When you have done this, further investigation will
show that there are really only a few hundred scores being played
anyway, thus narrowing down the possibilities immediately. Now if
you are the type that has a hard time remembering his own phone
number, you may get alarmed here unless you learn that (a) you
don't have to memorize it to conduct it, (b) as long as you can read
it from the score. Learning to read a score, of course, is not easy,
but it's something you just have to do, like wearing goggles if
you're a welder. And actually, don't even be baffled by the fact
that there are a few hundred around that get played, for of these
there is what is called "the standard" which is one that has been
played so much that orchestras don't even need to rehearse it any
more. Conductors do, but orchestras don't. And your task will be
a lead pipe cinch if you will go about it my way.

The first thing you do when you get to *your* town where it
is *your* orchestra and you are *their* conductor is to assume the stance
of a combination of Bismark, Mussolini, and the Grand Duke of

Serbia (the one they shot to get World War I started). At first everyone will think you are going to be another blitz from Berchtesgaden, when suddenly you demonstrate your love for democracy and the American way of life by announcing that you are going to conduct a poll. And then you send out a questionnaire asking *your* town what *they* would like your orchestra to play. You announce this in all the media (newspapers, radio, and TV, too, if you've had your teeth capped yet) and you say nice things about coordinating the efforts of the public schools with the cultural achievements of the community represented by *your* orchestra which *your* town is lucky enough now to have *you* conducting. This is called public relations.

Now considering the fact that only one-half of one percent of any town goes to Symphony Concerts (ever), you won't be bogged down too much with reading the answered questionnaires. In any event, throw them all away except for those of your board members and it will all boil down to about ten or twelve standard works of Beethoven, Brahms, Mozart, and Tschaikowsky. Not that they even really like those pieces, but they've learned to pronounce them themselves, you see, and don't want to waste the chance to work them into the conversation. This sort of musical name dropping is very popular especially among the ladies, and I have attended seances at Music Club Meetings (where they were communicating with the spirits of the long dead) and heard all kinds of exciting chatter about "portamenti" and "glissandi" done with such a dash that you would never have known that they had looked them up just before they came in to impress each other with. Sometimes when Dvorak is in season (yes, composers do go in and out of season like hats and gloves and button shoes) he gets mentioned because he wrote that lovely tune, you know the one, oh yes "Going Home." Very rarely do you hear any of these people actually say "I like the 3rd above all others—or I think the 6th is the most significant creation of our century." Come to think of it, though, I have heard some of their husbands express a great liking for the fifth.

So, neophyte or novice that you may well be, you will have plenty of companionship in those fringe-benefit music lovers who somehow like to talk about it more than they like to soak it up. So draw yourself up a list of all the music you know. Remember when you didn't know much, four scores and seven years ago? Look at you now, you have a huge collection of recordings and you've memorized Romeo and Juliet until you can conduct it backwards even. As a matter of fact, if you hadn't had your turntable fixed you might still be doing it that way. Divide the music you know by three years (which is the average tenure of a conductor anywhere) and then you will know exactly what your problem is in learning new stuff, or (as it is called in the trade) "preparing your season." Don't bother with concerti because the soloists have them all down pat anyway, and all you have to do is watch them like a hawk—especially during the curtain calls.

From the very beginning make these composers that you are conducting your very own. This is to say, refer to them as "My Brahms" or "My Mozart." Show this way that you have a vested interest in the matter so you can be scornfully contemptuous of "his Mozart" or "their Tschaikowsky." This way it will seem that YOU have the sole performance rights to the *REAL* Beethoven and the other guys are working only with cheap imitations. Somewhere along the line you can let it be known that the authorative approach to your own "reading" is exactly what the composer wanted. You can say that you studied this with a relative of the creator or a former student, or the composer in person. This will give you an unchallengeable position at all times. Just don't get careless and say you studied it personally with some joker that's been dead a long time. Always look up the birthdate of the composer and calculate your odds. In order to get familiar with this sort of thing, it may be even necessary for you to read a book or two on music history.

Your poll having been taken, you now publish the results of your findings which, by a strange co-incidence, just happens to be the ones which you are most familiar with yourself. You then print up a bunch of brochures announcing your season and send them out madly to other conductors all around the country. They are also doing the same thing, and while no one gets much out of it except the Post Office Department, occasionally you can find a mis-spelled word on one of theirs and show it around sneeringly. Since all of you are conducting virtually the same programs all the time (Beethoven and that group), you can show these around as if *they* copied everything you did. Don't forget to put on your programs "subject to change without notice" as this covers up a lot of bad judgment on your part and frequently comes in handy for eliminating the pieces which have five-four time in them.

A man needs at least two Beethoven Symphonies, one Mozart (41 is a pretty easy one to keep your place in), Tschaikowsky's 4th, Mendelssohn's Scotch, and Handel's Water Music. Caution: don't schedule the Scotch and Water on the same program if the WCTU is strong in your town. This music, plus Franck's "D Minor" and some symphonic poems like "Romeo and Juliet" by Tschaikowsky, "Till Eulenspeigel," by Strauss, and "The Afternoon Down on the Farm" by Debussy will give you a basic repertoire for a first season if there aren't too many concerts. If you need more, you can add one of the longer songs like Bach's "St. Matthew's Passion" and a batch of short encore pieces. When you add in what your soloists are going to play (Grieg, Tschaikowsky, or Schuman for piano and Mendelssohn, Sibelius, or Lalo for violin), you'll have quite a stack of numbers to write down as your "repertoire." You may want some overtures as curtain raisers like "The Marriage of Figaro," "The Bartered Bride," or one of the Rossini hits. Maybe a Wagnerian Overture, too, although they're better to finish programs with because they always end with a hell of a big bang and it gets lots of applause. I personally don't know of anything I would rather applaud than the end of an overture by Wagner. And, oh yes. Make sure that you make arrangements to have lots of rehearsals, for every thing you do that first year is going to be a world premiere. At least for you.

After you've been in the game for a while you can start sneaking a little contemporary music in every now and then, but don't over do it—why be half-safe when you can enjoy that womb-like warmth that the classics symbolize? Just keep remembering that board member who didn't like Chester Kovitch and that crowd. So give them a steady diet of Brahms, Beethoven, Tschaikowsky, and Mozart until you're either ready to change jobs or start repeating by popular request. If you don't like staying on in one town because of the necessity of having constantly to change the programs, you can always be a guest conductor. That way all you have to change is the towns.

Somehow it seems germane to me at this instant to insert a fragment from my vast biographical past since what I am about to tell you is so pertinent to the subject we are discussing. It has to do with repertoire in general and the three B's in particular and how I almost became one. A three-B that is.

Way back in 1945 when Dr. Frank Black was playing my Symphony No. 5 (yes, Virginia, there is really a number 5, too). Anyway, one day during a rehearsal of this predecessor to 5½, one of the 2nd violin players of the NBC Symphony Orchestra came up to me and told me that the boys in the orchestra were very much impressed with me as a composer and some of them were even saying that I was of genius stature.

I should have known by this time that he was exaggerating a mite when he mentioned genius, but one doesn't often get his head turned while at the same time he gets his leg pulled, so I listened to his pretty compliments in a state of agogery. (state of being "agog")

"Go on," I implored him imploringly.

"Some of the boys said to tell you," he went on, "that while the three B's used to be Bach, Beethoven, and Brahms, after playing your music they've decided that the three B's are now Bach, Beethoven and . . ."

"Yes, yes," I urged, "Bach, Beethoven, and . . ."

"That Bastard Gillis."

Well, talk about hitting an airpocket! I dropped even lower than what I thought he was for having told me. Later I learned that he was just a fun-loving fugitive from composition himself (with a slight burning-yearning for becoming a conductor, too) so I found it in my heart to forgive him because—even if I didn't get to be one of the three B's, I did get a pretty good yarn to pass along to you to illustrate whatever point it was that I was trying to illustrate. Legpulling, I think. Either that or repertoire.

"Repertoire" (and you may write this down as a definition) "is a word used in music which (while most people can't even spell it right, much less pronounce it) is necessary for you to have just in case anyone ever ask you if you know such and such a piece."

"Oh, sure" you can retort, "I've known it all my life."

Combine this with a shrug, a self-confident hoist of an eyebrow or so, and a quick-change of subject with an anecdote about some other piece altogether, and you have put yourself into a state of being admired within an inch of your life.

Now this definition is not Mr. Webster's, of course. His is somewhat confusing in that he says that: repertoire (rep-or-twar) is the complete list or supply of dramas, operas, pieces, or musical works available for performance." How drama got in there when we were distinctly talking about music, I'll never know. I can only assume that Webster wasn't paying attention, but I hope you are as the next word we are talking up is "repertory." For most normal human beings (among whom are a few of my friends and some graduate students) these two words ("repertoire" and "repertory") are interchangeable as to meaning and not only that, are generally pronounced the same way. But nay, not so. "Repertory" is pronounced "rep-ehr-tor-ee" rhyming with "si-si" (which is a phrase used by Mexican yes-men), and Mr. Webster defines it as "a place where something may be found."

So if someone asks you if something is in your "repertoire" (rep-or-twar), you can always reply that it is since (according to Webster, at least) a "repertoire" is only a list, even if it is not really in your head or "repertory" (rep-ehr-tor-ee) (rhymes with "oh, say can you SEE?" as in National Anthem) (ours).

Incidently, I've pretty much decided that this fellow Webster was a clever writer and a real gold-mine of information. Notice for instance, that before he ever even mentions "repertoire" or "repertory," he talks about "repercussion." Of the three, you need more "repertoire" than "repertory" and as for the latter, well, let the repercussion players have enough to go around for once.

Another thing I've been worried a good deal about lately is the rapid growth of the number of available conductors, most of whom (as we used to read in Billboard Magazine) seem to be "at liberty."

Conductors are one of those few commodities in over-supply that neither Roosevelt plowed-under nor Kennedy stockpiled, but what with all of this hue and cry for government subsidy of the arts, maybe we could get in a word about using the same system as is used by the Department of Agriculture in paying people to "not plant" cotton or to "not raise" wheat. This plan would call for government aid to communities to "not have" symphony seasons and would guarantee any conductor a good living if he "not" conducted. It appears on the surface like a good idea if they will also include a policy of "not having" girl drum majorettes and bands that dance during half-time at football games. This could include "not having" the announcer who explains what the hell it is that the band is trying to form out on the field which always ends up looking like a saggy circle anyway. If you'll write to your congressman, maybe we can get this problem taken care of and have nothing to worry about except how and where do you write to your congressman.

The only other solution I see for this undersupply of available podiums (or "podiae" if you've had Latin) is to specialize. Instead of a man being expected to learn his five and a half foot shelf of symphonic hits, we could restrict him to just one composer. He could be a Beethoven specialist and conduct nothing but Beethoven. If a local symphony orchestra wanted a little Beethoven on their program they could send for him. Of if that wouldn't still solve the enigma, we could cut him down to just one of Beethoven's symphonies which would give eight other guys one apiece to specialize in. Or you could go further and have them responsible for single movements (nine times four equals thirty-six (plus one extra one in the Pastorale) for Beethoven alone. And think of the possibilities in Haydn!)

A symphony concert using a Beethoven Symphony, the Brahms

*—maybe we could interest them in paying conductors
for "not" conducting.*

They need speeches about music—YOUR speeches.

"Variations on a Theme by Haydn" (one man per variation), and a big long suite like Tschaikowsky's "Nutcracker," would use up a raft of conductors in a single evening. Employment would reach an all-time high and think of all the chances the audience would get to applaud and all of those dress clothes you could sell. As for me, if this happens, I'll give up composition for good and go straight into the haberdashery business.

And critics! What a field day they could have with a multiple choice of criticizable potentials. This might even get bigger than pro football and auditoriums could be filled with whole sections of rooters and marching bands on stage during intermissions! Of coures, all of this may be just a wild dream (I *am* subject to spells now and then when I forget my Geritol). But it COULD happen. And something does have to happen to balance things out unless we force our music schools into a non-production schedule or arrange for CARE packages to be sent to these now-unemployed conductors, care of A.F. of M.

But it could go the other way entirely, which is why I am inserting this parable illustrating the fact—if you think the conductor has it good now—that it could get even better for him in his age of space and computers and instant oblivion. Scoff at it unbelievably if you will, but it was told to me by one Grover Ballondonck of RFD 3, Azle, Texas, the veracity of which he swore upon his family Bible (a Gideon he had taken on extended loan from the Baker Hotel in Dallas). It concerns Sir Humphrey Hogarth, the eminent Mexican Conductor, whose only words of English when he came to this country were "Si, Si."

He had been engaged to guest conduct the Little Rock Philanthropic and was an aghast conductor indeed when he learned that, because of certain problems of integration below the Mason-Dixon line, he would not be allowed to conduct any music with black notes in it before his all white-tie audience. *"C'est formidable"* he was heard to mutter in a foreign tongue as he hastily set out trying to figure out what to play that didn't have any black notes in it. He thought about transposing Chopin's "Black Note Etude" up a tone, but this would have made it a B-Tude and "B" has sharps in it which enharmonically could be construed as black notes by some of the more unmitigated.

Well, he wandered through his whole repertoire including "A Hunt in a Black Forest" and "Old Black Magic," and just about the time he had chewed the cork-tipped handle off of his best baton, the great idea hit him. He, Sir Humphrey in person, would write a concerto for himself.

Thus it came to pass (or verily, verily if you prefer), that the audience came to the concert and were astounded to see the stage dimly lighted except for a baby pink spot right over the podium. Draped loosely on an otherwise empty stage was a festoon of white velvet, in front of which sat two musicians, both hold shiny brass cymbals. And before the audience had scarcely quit gasping out of sheer surprise, Sir Humphrey mounted the podium and a hush fell as he raised his baton on the world premiere for "Concerto for Conductor, Single-handed."

For two hours and ten minutes he held them spellbound in his amazing exhibition of baton technique. At one point their mortal human eyeballs almost popped from their heads as he put the baton down to wend (swanlike with just a hint of elfin) through a slow movement that went from six-eight to three-four over five divided by two. In some passages, he even used decimals and he brought the whole evening to a close by conducting the finale with one hand tied behind his back.

When he had ended with his tired arms both pointing poignantly toward the podium, a yell ran rampant through the audience as they gave him a standing ovation and several people went home with their palms beaten to a pulp, so great was their joy! Next morning, the critic began his write-up with some words too big, even, to set in print.

"Silence" (he wrote) "is the most perfect form of music, especially where there is always the danger of those two damned cymbal players clanging out a loud one which they didn't."

He went on to describe the various movements and called the

cymbals "symbolic" of the "vast voids of sound unheard except by those as yet unborn." You know how critics get sometimes.

"Sir Humphrey" (he continued) "began the work in the Sistolic and Diasistolic Modes," and then he went on about how they all got goosebumps when "with a freezing gesture, he went into the Phyrgian." And the critic really raved about Sir Humphrey's parabolas and arcs and climaxed the whole review by comparing the podium to Mt. Everest which Sir Humphrey scaled musically like "A Knight on a Bald Mountain."

Anyway it was a smash, and Sir Humphrey was hired on the spot and now conducts all of the concerts except when the orchestra is there. Not too many attend anymore, however, for (as one fellow said) "if you've not heard it once, you've not heard it all!"

As we mentioned earlier, this story reeks of improbability, but does indicate how far a conductor could go if you let him. "Quiet Concerti, or: Variations on Silent Night" could become all the rage, especially for people who don't like music anyway. While we're waiting around for all of the big changes to happen though, we'd better get our nose to the grindstone, our shoulder to the wheel, and also hitch our wagon to a star. For until it all does come to pass, we have to learn to conduct some music just in case we ever get a chance to conduct it somewhere.

Anybody care to look at a score of mine?

CHAPTER VII

"Unaccustomed As I Am . . ."

Guisto Momento, a medieval monk who discovered that the only way to see while writing during the Dark Ages was to use illuminated manuscripts, is believed by some to have once said:

> "A man in ancient Greece trained himself to speak coherently by filling his mouth with rocks and standing at the seashore trying to out-shout the roar of the surf. In this way he became the most famous orator of his time. Go thou and do likewise!"

I am sure that none of you who went into this high calling of becoming a conductor ever dreamed that it was going to be anything but just conducting. The truth is now out. A conductor has many other things to do besides beating time and one thing which seemingly has very little to do with conducting (but which he has to do anyway) is making speeches. On the surface it doesn't seem that you, the Maharajah of Music in your town, should have to do any talking at all except maybe to the orchestra or occasionally at concerts where you explain to the audience why it is that you are not playing the piece which is printed on the program but instead you are substituting one which you already know. But just as any king has to speak sometimes to his subjects, you must also speak, and not only that, you have to do it well.

Ancient Greeks or not, we don't suggest that your basic training begin with filling your mouth with pebbles. In the first place, I don't want everybody calling any of *my* students "Mumbles," and in the second place, you don't need 'em. It's bad enough having rocks *in* your head.

So it's speechmaking for you and so kindly take notes as we go along as it will save you from untold embarrassments and besides, if you fail at conducting, you can always take up politics, preaching, or auctioneering. In any case, it won't be a total loss.

And since there isn't a single music school that I know of that has had the foresight and acumen to include this phase of your prepartion in its curriculum, be ever grateful that you were able to get the inside dope from me, your mentor and your friend. I may not be much else, but as a mentor, I can "ment" with the best of them. So: re-focus your glasses, memorize all the footnotes (if any), and glean it all, for (paragraphically speaking) a vision is about to unfold unto you that hasn't been observed much since shepherds watched their flocks by night.

"Why?" (you ask rhetorically) "should I have to make speeches? I am a conductor by trade and not a speechmaker!"

And I reply: "To get followers."

Conductors always have to have somebody following them and the trick is to have them also follow you outside the orchestra. So you make speeches to grow a cult, to cultivate disciples because you want and need people to love you and look upon you not only as Maestro but as Master. The quickest way to do this is from the speaker's rostrum. And your subject is music.

As we analyze a town (clinically) both anthropologically and socio-economically, we find there are several units which, for easier reading and more universal comprehension, we will here-in-after refer to as "groups." For a breakdown of our "groups" into their natural divisions, we will call them: (a) male, (b) female, and (c) assorted children. These are the three groups which will cry out for you to speak to them in your native tongue in what we lecture-experts call "speech form" or "the address." And once they get your address, they'll want your phone number for sure.

In the (a) or "male" group, you will find "men's clubs" most predominantly needful of your services. They are basically antagonistic (psychologically) as the average male still firmly believes that the arts (and artists) are slightly sissy, even though statistics galore have been assembled to prove that it takes more energy to play a symphony concert than it does to play a football game. Especially since the platoon system.

None-the-less, they'll still want you to speak because (a) they feel an obligation to soak up a little culture now and then so that they'll be able (later) to say to their friends: "We had Maestro McMangle at Rotary today and I don't want to brag, but I'll bet there weren't over three or four of us in the entire audience who had the faintest idea what he was talking about," and (b) men's clubs need speeches to fill up the time between the chicken a la king and the benediction.

We'll return later to discuss how to convert this group into being your disciples. In the meantime, let us examine the women in detail—metaphorically speaking, I mean.

As long as there are women there will be women's clubs and whether they are named the Santa Cecelia Society, the National Federation of Music Clubs, or Democrats for Mozart, they will be after *you*—the symbol of symphony—to speak to *them,* the cultural leaders of the arts in their communities.

Now these ladies, oppressed as they are by household tasks and childbearing, need to be inspired now and then by something more than vacuum-cleaning and frozen food-thawing. They need culture and they get their real kicks in life by listening to speeches about music. Many of them would rather hear a speech about Beethoven's music than to hear the music itself, actually, and you can't blame them, for quoting what you said about Beethoven is a heck of a lot easier than quoting the music he wrote. And if there is anybody in the world they like to quote, it's their very own symphony conductor, so go ahead and let them.

And too, like men's clubs, they are potential followers and remember that the hand that rocks the cradle rules the roost (as the saying goes). As a matter of fact, they are really your real followers and if you can keep them following and don't let them quite catch up to you, you're really king.

Group (c) are the children and while this is the hardest group to talk to as they squiggle and squirm about something fierce, they are important because *they* are your future followers and if you help them to learn to love music now, they are supposed to grow up and buy season tickets later. This is always a risk because this means that all of this work is wasted if you decide to change towns, but it is still a command as the Bible does tell us to suffer, the little children, etc.

Now that we have so cogently classified your audience (speech division) and have pointed out the importance of your public appearances in order to convert them to membership in your flock, it is time to take up what it is you will talk about and give a few helpful hints on platform patter that will insure your immediate success with one and all. And so let's take up first the "off the cuff, I didn't expect to be called on" informal-type talk as opposed to the "I will now deliver a scholarly lecture" kind.

This first type most often happens with group "A" (male) and group "B" (female) rather than with group "C" (kids) as the latter couldn't care less about you unless you happened to be a magician, an astronaut, or (if older) a Beetle. They are a separate category and we'll probe deeply into their little old mixed-up characteristics later, probably.

Suppose we begin with the men and you are at Rotary Club as a guest of the symphony chairman *and* the city's largest building contractor. Don't let the fact that he is a rich tycoon or still under indictment for defrauding the county government on that last courthouse he built, keep you from enjoying either the chicken a la king or the group-rendered song-cycle that always seems to include "When Arsh Eyes are Smallin'." You are introduced to the group by your host and instead of applauding you, they all holler out "Hi, Tom" or "Hi, Milt" or "Hi, Dimitri" or whatever your name is (and surely you must know that). You stand up and wave fraternally and the chairman says what an honor it is to have you and would you say a few words.

So, exuding a schoolboyish chagrin at being caught so impromptuly in such a disheveled state of mind, you take him up on it.

No matter what you say they won't really listen much as they haven't finished their Nesselrode or Brown Betty yet, so just say that it is *you* who is being honored and you look forward to seeing them at your concerts this season. Never, never extemporize a better speech than the one about to be given by the local chief of police who is going to talk on: "Crime can be fun." And don't take up too much time, either, because all these guys works for a living and have to get the hell back to their office the minute the benediction is amened. Just say thanks and sit down. Later on they'll agree you made a fine impression and ask you what line of work was it you said you were in. And within a fort-night (two weeks in London) (ah, London!) they will ask you back to give the main talk. There is time enough to convert them all from apathy to enthusiasm when you'll have their undivided attention. All except for the fellow who introduces you who is still working on his Nesselrode, Brown Betty, or (as chairman) maybe even some lemon Jello.

For this type of speech, determine in advince just what it is you want them to think of you as: God of Music or Ordinary Mortal! The best approach is a touch of both so that they can see you've descended from your throne to mingle among them and they'll appreciate that. Prepare your subject well (which should be easy because it will be YOU) and get to their all-male hearts with a joke that will enable them to emphathize immediately and be able to tell folks later "he's a regular guy, conductor or not."

You are (you tell them) just like they are: an executive of a business called music. If there's one thing a man likes to be known as, it's being an executive and he'll warm up to you right away, probably never ever thinking about the fact that *your* business goes into the red year after year no matter what you play.

You are also(you continue) in show business. This will give them something to think about as they really hadn't thought of it that way before. They'll like the idea as there is no business like show business as the song says.

And what you want to do today (you point out) is to invite them backstage as while there is no business like show business, you should see what goes on backstage if you really want to be in the inner circle.

Everyman likes to be "in" on something and the fact that you're letting them all in at the same time probably won't be noticed as you tell them spicy little tidbits like how the cello got its "F" hole, how the Sousaphone was born, or what Berlioz and Mendelssohn fell out about back in Chapter One of this very same book. You can tell them that the combined cost of all the instruments in your orchestra compares favorably with their own expenses (deductible) and you can mention that the combined cost of the education of all of your players is staggeringly astronomical like their taxes and if there's anything we need in this country right now it is a good tax reform that gives a man an even chance at least to re-coup his investment and make a reasonable profit (applause). You thus let them know that you're a business man, really, and up to now they had no idea. And since business is business, they might even learn to like music a little. At least they all promise themselves privately that they'll try it once and if they don't like it they can always take it back.

With this sort of dynamism in speaking their jargon and putting your art within the framework of their socio-economic comprehension, you will have won them over completely and that's when you can start talking to them about tax-deductible contributions to your own business and remember that you're really helping them because all business men need deductions and it might as well be you.

The main thing in talking to men is to emphasize that what you are doing is just as male as bank-presidenting or football-coaching, that your work is as masculine as stock broking or merchandising —and keep insisting over and over that, by golly, yours is the only business in the whole world that isn't being taken over by women, bless 'em, but composers and conductors from time immoral have been men—not women, and it's going to stay that way because if God had wanted women to be conductors and composers He would have said so in the Good Book.

And conclude the whole thing by personally inviting their club to be your guest at the first concert as a trial offer. And say that a group that sits together proves that the American system of free enterprise and democracy is here to stay together.

At that point, sit down.

There is no need here to describe tumultous applause and emotion-wracked audience. You will experience this all yourself. In passing, let me say how sorry I am that (of all the forms of art) no one has ever been able to devise an appropriate encore in public speaking. Just know, however, that if it were possible, your speech would have got one. For with this talk you will have converted them all—maybe not to music itself, but at least to talks about music which is the next best thing.

Your next triumph will be the ladies. For you will be invited to address them or lecture them or make them a talk just on the basis that you are what you are, which is "Maestro" capital "M." And they'll adore you, for there's nothing the lady's club set would rather do to you while you're making them a talk than adore you. You may get the feeling on such an occasion that you're facing a whole roomful of Botticelli models auditioning for the "Adoration of the Magi" but don't let it throw you. Adore them right back and rightfully so, as the hand that rocks the cradle also signs the checks and your orchestra can always use a check.

For the ladies, your approach has to be geared feministically. They like to know things like the true story of Beethoven's Moonlight Sonata and why Haydn's wife used his music to line the bottom of her cake pans when she baked. They'll titter deliciously at veiled references to illicit love and blush prettily to talk involving mistresses. Why the hell a composer's mistress is any more interesting than a plumber's friend is beyond me, but the fact is, it is. Actually you should intimate (for the church crowd) that you don't approve of this, but if mistressing ever did come back into style again you couldn't think of anybody you'd rather illicit with than them. If you say this with contact lenses they'll all think you're focusing straight at them and being misty-eyed while doing it.

Tell them stuff about deprivations and poverty that the masters had to put up with, too. There won't be a dry eye in the house as you mention garrets and slums and such that some of the biggest composers in the world have lived in. In passing, let me say that there's one big danger in all of this war on poverty that President Johnson is carrying on right now—it may stamp out composers completely.

Mention Beethoven's aloneness and how he had to take out his own garbage, tell about Schubert and how he was secretly in love with some princess or other and say that that's probably why he didn't finish that unfinished symphony and can you blame him? Describe Handel and how he had to practice his harpsichord by moonlight and be sure to mention Rimski's hyphenation for Korsakov. You can see their imaginations soar as each in turn empties Beethoven's garbage can or sews a button on Moussorgsky's tattered greatcoat. The same woman wouldn't normally stoop to darn a sock or rake the yard for her own husband, but will secretly yearn (in her deepest heart) for the rich privilege to have lived when one could have done dishes for Debussy or scoured pots and pans for Puccini.

"Oh, to have been a part of all that," they'll sigh romantically, refusing even to think about their own sinkfuls of breakfast plates and hampers filled with dirty shirts at home.

You can, with such excursions into the private lives of those men of music, tittilate them (the women, I mean) into such a state that they won't bother you with such foolish questions as "what is a counterpoint?" or "when was the grace note invented?" during the question-answer period. They will have been transported beyond such planetary limitations. And if you really want to send them into spasms of delight, lecture them on opera.

A woman who would slap your face if you told her an off-color story privately will pant like a bad case of dry heaves if you tell her publically how the Duke in this opera raped the King's daughter after having had an illegitmate child by his brother's wife, while secretly running a white slavery ring for the Princess who ate her lovers alive, one by one. And that's just Act I—wait until you hear what happened in Act III.

You (unlike those dirty shirts) are unhampered and, with imagination and not too much conscience, you can fill their hearts with rapture, all the while serving your cause in building yourself a real live-wire bunch of slaveys for committees, concerts, and contributions.

"But what of kids?" you ask, dreading the day you'll have to talk with them. Well, most of the time you are protected from physical harm by the teachers in the schools you have so ill-advisedly consented to speak at, and generally it isn't too long anyway because class periods are short. It is the Children's Concert for which you must prepare with infinite care. For here you must speak to a whole auditorium filled with a thousand or so kids, all of whom look like St. Vitus Dance patients who have just been dusted copiously with itching powder.

You are on your podium and they are in their seats and in the aisles and on the floor and throwing paper space ships (formerly airplanes) from the balcony and doing everything else that the products of our homes in an enlightened age do and I'll tell you, kids didn't act like that when I was a kid, no sirreee! You quiet them down by signalling for a fanfare of brass and percussion especially designed to shatter their twitchy little eardrums. They notice it right away and look in your direction. You say:

"Hello children!"

And they'll yell back:

"Hello Micetro"

For if there's anything kids like to do at Children's Concerts more than to have it over with even, it's to yell. So take advantage of this and ask them who their favorite composer is.

"Beethoven" they'll yell back. Not that he is, understand, but this is what their teachers told them to yell to you when and if you asked them to. Of course, the whole thing will end up sounding more like a pep rally than a concert, but it'll at least give you a chance to play a few short pieces and the music teachers will all beam as their kids recognize the theme from the "Unfinished Symphony" by the song they taught them with words that go:

'This is the one I wrote
Which critics say I never fin-ished
But then, if you will note

Its name and fame have not dimin-ished.

Ha Ha, the joke's on you.

I always quit when I am thru-oo, etc."

Well, you'll have to admit it's better than the words they use with "Anitra's Dance."

The main thing at Children's Concerts is to encourage the children to grow up and come to the grownup concerts with their daddies and mommies in the meanwhile. I think that's the main purpose. Anyway, it'll do until they do grow up and you get a chance to tell them finky little stories and play their dinky little pieces and get adored by the teacher whose little monsters you have taken off her hands for at least a few minutes. And if you're a teacher every little bit helps.

So now I hope you see how much you have been guided and pre-pared for that phase of your career which is of equal importance to your podium power, i.e. the ability to speak a speech at the drop of a gavel. Just as the bedside manner is vital to a medical man, your suave acceptance of the dangers of after dinner speeches and tea festivals at music clubs must be equally evidential of the power that lies within you. And I know that you can do it, for anybody that conducts Brahms the way you do can certainly talk about him better.

From here on out, you're on your own. As I mentioned earlier, a little learning is a dangerous thing, but not nearly as much as menus at men's club luncheons and music clubs banquets.

Anyone for chicken a la king?

CHAPTER VIII (or have eaten)

"But It Said In The Paper..."

Nowhere in the jungle of the arts is there more evidence of the unremitting conflict between man and beast than in the age-old battle between conductor and critic. It is as if you were the beast (which you aren't at all, as everyone who knows you will can testify) and as if he (the critic) were the great White Hunter eternally following your spoor with typewriter in hand, paragraphing you into submission and adverbing you to extinction as metaphors and similes shower down upon you like re-entry nose cones. I hope there will be a few among you who will notice the skillful syntax here and will marvel, yea even be confounded by my insight into my subject. And say "hear, hear." I can only acknowledge such tributes modestly and say that it is only my own vast experience with the subject and a much-thumbed nose that enables me to write with such perpiscacity and honesty.

And speaking of spoors being followed, it may be that of the two of you, the critic (or great White Hunter) leaves a more permanent trail than you do. After all, *his* is in print and yours is only echoed dimly in the mind's inability to recall in exactitude. Your position is debatable while his is indelibly (not really, but it is more exciting to write it this way) imprinted in the annals of time's own morgue, yesterday's newspaper. When *you* have finished *your* work, *his* work has only begun.

But let us define. I always feel that when we get into a subject as large as this we should have something firm and fast to hang on to, especially if we are going to keep up our high standards of intelligent

*Determine in advance just what it is you want your
audience to think of you as—.*

There are some thinkers—who say that critics got started back in the days when kings had jesters and commanded them to give a report on the concerts.

investigation. I'm personally going to use my small Webster's dictionary, as I don't have the strength for the large one which could give you a hernia even to lift, let alone look up anything in. Mine is the handy collegiate one, bound in my own college colors. Turn with me, if you will, to page 240 of the 5th edition and the first word you'll run across is "Cretinism" which Webster slyly puts in there having probably had some trouble along the way with critics himself. However, we locate the word we're after (which is *critic,* remember?) and we find: *"one who expresses a reasoned opinion on any matter, involving a judgement of its value, truth, or an appreciation of its beauty or technique; one given to harsh or captious judgment; a caviler or carper; one skilled in judging the merits of literary or artistic works."* I hastily interject here that all you book critics must understand that I'm writing about *music* critics and I have nothing but the highest regard for every single one of you. (You have to put stuff like this in, folks, or you'll get clobbered.)

Webster goes on to also define *"Critique"* which is what critics call what they come out with. It is (and I quote verbatim) *"a critical estimate of a work or literature or art."* I'm sure that the fact that Webster has listed as his next word *"croak; a low, hoarse noise in the throat; to grumble, to forebode evil"* was not merely an accidental placement for as I mentioned even dictionary writers are human and have to lash out once in awhile.

A critic, then, is one who criticizes, and in the case of a music critic he criticizes music whether with a low, hoarse grumble of foreboding evil or critiqued in print in somebody's newspaper. Generally he gets paid for it (if it is in print) although usually not much—and it is as much an occupation to him as say, embalming would be to an undertaker or as moonshooting would be to an astronaut.

Here I would like to quote a fragment of a letter from my mother who wrote to me about some art works long treasured by my family ever since I wrote them.

"Dear Son" (she begins informally) "don't be upset about what those *word merchants* are saying about you in their columns, and especially about your music. I'm sure you'll agree with me that their vocabularies consist generally of evasive phrases, time-worn cliches, and seldom-used compliments. Pay no attention to them as time will prove who is right. P.S. I'll send along your scrap book in a few days."

Mom was speaking about critics and composers, but our problem here is not composers; it is conductors of which one of them is you or will be as soon as we finish educating you up to it. And since the critic will always be a powerful force in your life, especially since he can rouse the rabble against you, I am beholden as everything to tell you all I know about them to help you put on the whole armour of truth in your death-throe duel with the only man standing between you and immortality. Besides yourself, that it.

While the pen may not be mightier than the sword, it does outrank the baton and so we must gird up our loins the better to be able to cope with this untidy situation which prevails, i.e. the music critic. And since we really want to dig into the whole subject academically and leave no term unstoned, we'll research the past to see from whence they came, historic-like. And so we won't go too far astray from our subject, we'll start with them where we started with you. At the beginning.

It is said that the inventor of the wheel got his idea from watching critics as they were always around. Others say that the critic appeared as an art function a split second after the first conductor was born. I personally feel that it was the first composer, but I may be jaundiced. At any rate, with the very first downbeat by the first conductor, there was a loud howl of "I don't like it" and immediately the stonechips flew as the man with the chisel pounded his very first critique into the Rosetta Stone of time—or whatever the daily paper of the period was called. It must have been better in those days of clay tablets or rock writing, for at least you could throw them at the critic with some chance of inflicting bodily damage. After all, what critic ever got injured in our day by being clubbed by a newspaper—even the Sunday Times?

But as I was saying, first the downbeat and then the objection. And in that immortal moment of time, the world was divided in twain—critic versus everything (including conductors) in a sort of half-past destiny that persists, yea, even unto this present day. *Selah.* (as they say in the Bible.)

There are some thinkers (musicologists—to name a few) who hold that it was kings and such who started it all. Kings hired orchestras and composers (who needed royalties even in those days) and insisted that they produce music to while away long kingly evenings, but actually the kings were so busy kinging that they didn't have time to find out if they were getting their money's worth. And so since they always had a jester around that they could trust, they asked them. One could, with a few extra words and an unbridled imagination, re-create the scene.

It is evening at the King's palace and a gala concert is scheduled for along about the venison and stuffed pig course. The king has been in his counting house all day and is just plain worn out from taxing his serfs and vassals—you can understand this, I'm sure, as it could happen to anybody. He was tired and his crown didn't fit and he just wasn't up to this festive occasion of the state visit of his uncle Emperor Thorax the Third. The musicians, all thirty of them, rose from their places below the salt and moved into position to play, their eyeballs red from poor light and woodsmoke that erupted uninterruptedly from the massive fireplace on which there was a spit. But it would have taken more than spit to put out that fire as it roared away at the Yule logs constantly fed to it.

The musicians were under the direction of Mynheer Frimple (who was also the court composer) and they looked forward dimly to the whiplash circumventions that passed for conducting in those days.

The king belched softly and beckoned his jester, Gimpy the Tone Deaf, to approach his throne.

"Varlet," said the King but in a foreign language that would send you skittering to a dictionary looking it up if I didn't translate it for you.

"Varlet, prithee keep thine ear open and give me word if this be good or naught. I have a strange suspicion that this knave doth palm off watered-down Bach and Buxtehude on me."

"Oh hang it, King," the jester replied, "I have to do everything around this cotton-pickin' castle." But he did it anyway because jesting jobs were hard to come by.

"What hath Groves Dictionary of Musick to say of this man who scrives my jots and tittles" croaked (or "grumbled in a low, coarse voice foreboding evil") the king.

But there was no answer as the jester had dozed off in a fit of stupor brought on by not wanting to hear the music lest it affect his judgment.

The concert finished and the musicians put down their brand new Stradivari (plural) and waited for the king to re-act. He, in a fit of carelessness which later led people to refer to him (in history) as "Sacks the Stupid" had put his hand into the fireplace and was now busily engaged in trying to put his fingers out by beating his hands together. That was, as far as we know, the first applause because when he did it, everybody else did it although it wasn't until later that it was decided unnecessary to set your fingers on fire first.

Well, the King looked at Gimpy (the tone deaf) and Gimpy's thumbs were down in the age-old gesture of condemnation. The King asked him to put it in writing and that night, a Knight who was town-crier, cried out the critique from a scroll which Gimpy had scribed personally. It began:

"Now hear this!"

"Tonight in Skullbrake Hall, the King's own orchestra played Mynheer Frimple's Serendipity Symphony. Mynheer lost all the way around.

Not only was his music bad, it was played badly. And since he was the conductor too, it's a toss-up where the darts and slings of this critique ought to be hurled. Or it would be if Mynheer Frimple was still with us. But, alack, he's not!

For one of the highlights of the evening was when Emporer Thorax gave King Sacks the gift of a new conductor, Homer the Homely. This happened right after the King had hanged Mynheer Frimple as an encore to the Serendipity. The audience applauded wildly and the King announced that Frimple would be missed, but not by the orchestra."

I could go on and on, but even an unbridled imagination gets tired now and then.

Now I'm not saying that it really happened this way, understand, but it could have and nobody can say for sure that it really didn't. Not even musicologists, right fellows? What we do know though is, that after newspapers came into being there was always some joker (formerly jester) who got the job as music critic. And the more conductors and composers there were, the more critics. Aldous Lirg in his tome "After Groves, What?" suggested that the only way to get rid of them is to get rid of what causes them—music. Composers and conductors still hope for a general plague (such as might be contracted from hanging around a verbiage disposal plant) to descend upon music critics as a sort of universal judgement. If not that, they can always hope for mass "criti-cide."

Critics by and large are generally forced into their occupations by editorial circumstances. They would much rather watch a good six-alarm fire, a plane crash, or an execution than be trudging up to Carnegie Hall or Lincoln Center all the time, but because some grouchy-bastard-of-an-editor forces them to cover concerts, they in turn are forced to get even with somebody and the general result is your problem.

But make no mistake. They don't take up music criticism because they *can't* conduct, perform, or compose. Not at all! I don't believe this for one moment and have no doubt that, given *your* chance (or if they really wanted to) they could out-conduct you any day of the week and twice on Sunday. And they could even out-compose me with a little more talent and some native ingenuity. They just *don't* do these things because they have dedicated their lives to knowing all there is to know and by God, they're not going to waste it on *just* being a performer when they can do infinitely more world-good by writing about it.

So no disrespect, please. You as a conductor, will be better served if you place it all in proper perspective and learn to live with it. They're here and they're going to stay. The only way to get rid of critics is to get rid of newspapers and then how would we start the campfire? So let them write what they please and if it's about somebody else, enjoy it. And if it's about you, well, you can always resort to "did you ever hear of anybody putting up a statue to a critic?" The fact that no one ever has put one up of you has nothing to do with it. Say it anyway.

There is always a sort of primitive mating dance that takes place during the early part of your career as a conductor in the critic's town and it involves you and him. We authorities call this the "nesting" period and it is not until you have laid an egg that the next period starts. You'll know when it's over because he ceases the serenades and starts typing with a guillotine.

At first he'll review you with "we prefer to wait and see" attitudes and "we make allowances for this first concert because" or "after all, he had only received the score late yesterday afternoon and . . ." Now this is all for the best and so far, it's in your favor. Later when his festerings become more feverish with comparisons such as "I have never been contented with Mozart since Maestro X did such a brilliant exposé of it last season as guest conductor. . . ."

This can mean two things—either that he just isn't contented with Mozart anymore at all, or that he likes Maestro X better than he likes you. In the latter case, just shrug. You'll need to work on a good shrug and this takes practice but you can, with the proper endeavor, shrug such a shrug that it looks for all the world like you were saying "I couldn't care less" and by dropping the clavical a little lower you can imply (or infer) "what does that guy know about music or even conducting?" It is always well, too, to be able to grimace. A grimace is sort of a Mona Lisa smile in reverse, a sort of "take the tooth out, doc, to hell with saving the nerve" expression. Wonders can be done with grimace and shrugs, especially when timed properly (as when a critic's quote is being read to you) or done with little or no humility.

While the nesting season is going on, you'll probably meet the critic at some soirré or other so don't get angry. After all, he's only human too and both of you are in rather odd occupations. Just be careful. Be reserved without being stiff (for heaven's sake never get stiff with a critic, no telling what you might call him, fortified by alcohol). Just be aloof. That's enough. We can well imagine such a conversation as this might result from your first encounter. You shrug and grimace (but pleasantly) (turn Mona back over) and extend your hand.

"It's a real pleasure," you say, "I have certainly heard about YOU in this town."

This will bother him temporarily because he doesn't know for sure what you mean by it. You proceed.

"I've read a lot of your reviews and your command of the language is fabulous." Down deep in your heart you know you're lying and he knows you're lying and you know he knows you know you're lying, but this will please him anyway. He'll probably even beam a little for if there's anything he'd rather hear even than he really known his business, it's that he really commands the language. He shrugs a little (probably takes from the same shrug teacher that you go to) and starts to reply but you interject.

"May I freshen your drink?"

He'll peer at you myopically through his thick-lensed glasses to see if he can see if you're really sincere or if you've heard the current rumor that he's such a lush that he thinks that when the oboe blows the note to tune up the orchestra that he's playing double-A.

You signal for a pair of martinis and he begins in on you.

"Do you know any of the works of Praetorius Gebhardt, circa 1626?" He has you, for to admit ignorance marks you as unschooled. But you can't afford to say yes or he's liable to ask you to whistle a theme or so. So instead you say:

"Not too well—ever since I read ———— . . ." and here you insert the name of a world-renowned critic whose authority can't be challenged, especially by a piddlewacker on the local gazette like him. He'll get your point and shift the subject around to festivals.

"When I was at the Gezunheit Plotz last summer to hear the entire Mahler, Beethoven, Wagner, Haydn, Mozart, and Frimple cycle, I had a chance to verify for all time . . ."

He's warning you that he knows how all these pieces go and if you play them he'll recognize them instantly. So you reply:

"Ah yes, it *was* wonderful. Strange we didn't bump into each other . . ."

It really isn't strange at all, come to think of it. He was at Aspen and you weren't back from conducting college yet where you had gone for a quick refresher course in trilogy. Three martinis later, your conviviality engendered by gin and vermouth, you have both settled down to panning *other* conductors and *other* critics and you both decide that each of you is a great guy no matter what anybody says. At least until the gin wears off. But the nesting season ends when he plucks enough of your pinfeathers to make a warbonnet for his head as he sets out after your music scalp because you didn't play Brahms and Frimple at the same speed he learned it from that microgroove LP that whoosis put out in '33. And not only that, he called your Strauss "senile," your Beethoven "boring," and your Debussy "dull." Well, at least he called them yours!

As a general summary to this chapter, just let me say that you can't win because he has a newspaper. Oh, you can write articles, get on panels, go on the radio, and even make remarks at women's clubs about the need for at least a grammar school education for some people you could mention. But it is of no avail. This is one place where even your capped teeth won't help you on TV. The critic always wins because he has the last word.

And when he finally does win and you pack your suitcase with its sequin-studded baton and tails that glow in the dark, just know that you're really lucky at that. If it hadn't been for some other critic in the new town you're going to that job wouldn't be vacant either.

So don't "cavil" or "carp" at him, don't croak at him in a grumbly voice foreboding doom, don't vituperate—just edit him down to your advantage and eat yogurt for your ulcer. When he writes about you that "his Brahms should have soared etherially in exotic metamorphasis," get out your pencil and "X" out the "should have" and you'll have a real nice review for your scrap book: "His Brahms soared etherially."

Who can ask for more? Especially if he spelled your name right.

"I have certainly heard about YOU in this town."

*—music got invented when some caveman accidently
banged a stone club up against a hollow tree trunk—.*

CHAPTER IX

From Serpents To Sackbuts

There is this yarn about the neophyte conductor whose principal qualifications for being on the podium was the fact that his daddy was a rich millionaire and very indulgent. Actually he didn't care what the kid did, he just wanted to keep him out of the family business. And so, although this fellow was so musically untutored that he scarcely knew his brass from his oboe, he traded banknotes for an opportunity to make musical ones and soared to the podium with all the zestful grace of a gooney bird. Success (just like in Horatio Alger's "Bound to Rise") had at long last come to him, despite his background of hardship and troubles by the millions.

He called out the first number at rehearsal, "Heart Wounds," a little opus by Grieg commissioned by the AMA, but due to his tendency to mumble (he couldn't help it because he had been born with a silver spoon in his mouth), only the strings understood him and the bass drummer (formerly a pile-driver operator whose biceps was one quivering mass of unused muscle) came in with such a hell of a bang on the downbeat that the conductor waved the proceedings to a stop and looked around bewilderedly, saying:

"Now who did that?"

Well, at least he noticed!

All of this is a prelude to the fact that, sooner or later, we're going to have to learn which one is which, and while most books would have pictures of all the instruments in them for your erudition, we'd rather just tell you all about the subject and let it go at that. But first, how did it all get started?

Legend has it that the first music came before mankind (and his friends, womenkind) had even learned to talk, and that from the first singing sounds which they made, during lullabies and love songs (or vice versa), words were fashioned. So even though it is a little hard to believe that music came before language, you'll just have to take my word for it that it did. I couldn't prove it, but it's just one of those things you know. Maybe that's why they have you study music by using syllables, which everybody knows are what words are made up of. The first instrumental music was supposed to have started with the great god Pan who happened to be standing in a swamp or somewhere where rushes and reeds grow, and he heard the wind whistling over their open tops and the sound it made was so nice that he thought he would invent the Pan Pipes. I hold to the theory myself that it happened when some cavemen accidentally banged a stone club up against a hollow tree trunk and the boom sounded so good he invented the drum. There are other theories, too. In the Bible, for instance, you are always reading about bands of angels who played nothing but harps, although in some paintings, I've seen one of them about to blow a trumpet. And one ancient tapestry has some trombones in it (*sackbuts* they were called back then). However, these angels were flying downhill at the time, so maybe they weren't in the same union with the harp and trumpet ones.

Anyway, Pan cut off a bunch of reeds of different lengths and stopped up one end and then blew across the top, not only inventing the first instruments, but the scale too. He made them too large at first, but was able to make them smaller by washing them in some brand "X" detergent and thus, the "syrinx." Or at least that's what I was told in the third grade by a lady who was always honking around with a pitch pipe to get us started singing "Good morning to you, good morning to you, we're all in our places with sunshiny faces." We also had a great one called "Cherries are ripe, cherries are ripe, the robin sang one day." This one confused me no end because I used to skulk around our orchard back in Cameron, Missouri days trying to catch one of them doing it. I never did, but maybe it was because we raised apples and I guess it's harder for robins to say "Apples are ripe." Let's see, where were we? Oh yes, the great god Pan and his pipes.

Pan was a Greek god you know, and the Greeks have been given a lot of credit for bringing music up to the status of an art. They had a lot of instruments that they played together in groups, although history does not relate whether or not they ever sounded very good. There was a 15-stringed lyre (or kithara) which was supposed to be great for playing the Dorian or Hypo-lydian modes on, but it would take a fellow with mighty long arms to handle one of these jobs from some of the pictures I have seen. Maybe they just said they played them and that's why we call them lyres.

After the Greeks came the Romans, and since they were world conquerors, they brought in rebecs from India, gongs and cymbals from Turkey, and sampans from China. They also had a lot of brass instruments (as all warlike people do). You can't fight a good war on muted second violins, you know! And they had conclaves of these musicians who played for the gladiators and Christian massacres. I had a teacher once who claimed that the reason we, in the western world, use the diatonic major scale, is because the Romans used so much brass that our ears became tuned to the overtone system inherent in brasses. Not that I dispute him, but I don't think it's that way at all. I think we use it just because it's around and handy.

However, with the Fall of the Roman Empire by Gibbons, instrumental music was banned by the church which was the first time band music came along. Choral music (or singing) took over and there is a lot of interesting stuff on this around if you want to look it up for telling people about later. There is nothing quite as impressive as to be able to casually mention people like *Hucbald the Elder* or *Odo of Cluny* and then explain the Guidonian Hand and its influence on the plagal cadence. Anyway, choral music went on a lot during what is now called the Dark Ages and about the only players around were guys like the minstrels. These are not the "Mr. Interlocutor" kind, but were rather traveling lute and lyre players whose main living was king entertaining. But choral music finally got out of hand when they invented opera and so this called for orchestras, probably to help drown out the singers.

The first orchestras had all sorts of oddball instruments in them including bombards and serpents. In those days when some leader saw serpents in his orchestra, it wasn't necessarily because he had been drinking cheap gin. He really saw them! But they, like many of the other ancient instruments, couldn't put out much volume and so one by one they got replaced by louder things. Things were pretty disorganized and there was no standard instrumentation at all as we now have with our own symphony orchestras. It must have been more like it is with bands now, with one town having 70 serpents (what a pit it would take for *them* to hiss in), 19 sackbuts, and one bombard, while the next town might have had a bunch of clavichords and harpsichords plus a whole covey of recorders and rebecs and lutes. Some groups had nothing but strings (pronounced "strangs" in Dallas) and others would have so many woodwinds and brasses you could hardly hear the people talking while the music was being played.

George Frederick Handel (circa) loved oboes and sometimes used as many as forty at a time. The plural of that word is "Oboi" and may have been coined by Handel who is quoted to have said: "Oh boy, look at all the oboes!"

The whole thing finally settled down as kings grew poorer and unions got stronger and so today a symphony orchestra is roughly divided into four sections, not counting you and the harpist. These are (a) strings, (b) woodwinds, (c) brasses, and (d) percussion. And if you think you can get it explained any better than that, Buster, well I'd like to see it myself.

One of the best ways for you to tell which is which if you're not really sure, is to come into the first rehearsal with what looks to be a blueprint, but which is really a seating chart of the orchestra provided to you by your librarian. But don't even trust him, because anyone less than a conductor can be pretty sneaky sometimes and everybody (including your own brother) is probably trying to get your place on the podium. So check this out by saying something like:

"Will the French Horns change places with the Violas?" Now

if THEY know who THEY are, then you're okay. Don't ever get cute and say "Will the real first oboe please stand up?" as they will then *know* you don't know, and if there is anything *worse* than not knowing, it is having *them* know that you *know* that they *know* that you don't know.

The French Horns, by the way, are those fellows who are always turning their instruments over and over to drain the water out of them. Generally they do this just after they've blooped an entrance and then they look at their horns as if the whole thing were its fault, disappointed at it for having let them down at a time like this. You can tell the clarinets, because when they make a mistake they always blow furiously on the keys like it had just caught on fire or something. Trombone players always duck down behind the stands when they goof, so if you're looking for them, just look around for what seems to be empty seats. String players are the ones with the bows who are either always winding them up (the bows) when you want to get their attention or else a string breaks magically for them in the middle of the toughest part. Rumor has it that they all have a small sawed-off Gem razor blade taped to their thumb just to insure this sort of thing happening. Locating all of the instruments wouldn't be too tough if you will keep up this game of musical chairs for a few days, like moving the oboes to where the trumpets sit and so on. If they get nosey, you can always explain it with: "I've been dissatisfied for years with the standard seating arrangements in orchestras and feel that the balance can be improved and so forth and so on and on . . ." Pretty soon you'll have it all straight unless you get invited to direct a band.

Let me put in a paragraph right here about the subtle difference in the use of the terms "direct" (when applied to bands) and "conduct" (when used for orchestra). I think the main difference in this caste system of terms stems from the fact that the orchestra has so many string players in it, each and every one of them equipped with a bow which can be converted into a baton in the twinkling of an eye. Therefore, you have to *conduct yourself* with the greatest of skill to outwit these instant Ormandys, none of whom would hesitate for a moment to trample the others to death in the race to the podium if you ever left it untended once. Never leave a podium except during intermissions or at the end of a rehearsal or concert, because there's many an anxious guy who just knows he can do it better than you can and he has no compunction (either) about the way he gets there. If you have to leave, say "King's X" like you used to do in "Hide and Seek" and this automatically puts them on their honor while you're gone. Either that or take it with you.

Some musicologists who are licensed by the state claim that "to conduct" is a verb which once was the same verb used when they annointed kings and such, while "to direct" is more like for showing people where the restrooms are. I don't hold with this, however, I am not licensed by the state so we may have to take their word for it. Everybody knows what a curious switch in the meaning of words has taken place somewhere along the line, however, or how come a member of the Board of Directors of the New York Central Railroad outranks the conductors? Some folks think it has something to do with the costume worn—in case of conductors, black (and as such) more related to death, witchcraft, or magic. Band directors wear gaudy uniforms with gold braid and tassels (yea, even plumes yet!) and many times look more like doormen at swank night clubs or musical comedy generals than musicians. One band director I heard of in San Diego was so uniformed up one night that seven Ensigns saluted him and escorted him on board a battleship and he was four weeks out to sea before he could finally convince them that he was only the assistant band leader at Santa Monica Junior High.

Sometimes I think that the problem of names exists because the bands march and the orchestras don't and that the term "director" got used because it is really the drum major who leads the band (he's the fellow in the tall hat who is always tripping over the 30 yard line) and the director just "directs" where they are to march. Most band directors want to be orchestra conductors, but they are so handicapped because they have to spend so much time supervising study hall and teaching twirling to wiggly majorettes, that they usually don't have too much time to take up music. Maybe this book will help them to.

So if you are invited to "direct" a band, don't start conducting at it, for they're not used to this and it will confuse them right off the bat. You might remember to invite the local band director to your podium for a return match sometime in case you've got a march you'd like to have played or want to get in good with the school crowd so you can sell more tickets to the Youth Concert. Remember that there are no strings in the band, so if you see some, you have gone to the wrong room for rehearsal and so go on down to the gym. That's where they generally have to practice. Orchestras "rehearse" but bands "practice." It's like the difference between doctoring and undertaking. The doctors *practice* but it's the morticians who *conduct* the funerals. So, having noticed that there are no strings you must also notice that a band has a bunch of extra instruments in it plus more of the same kind you've got in your group, except some of them are funnier looking. In your group, it's the people who are funnier looking generally.

Beginning with usually about thirty flutes (mostly girls who took it up because trombones and tubas are heavier to carry around and don't fit the school locker as well), you'll see whole flocks of instruments that have long necks on them and look for all the world like skinny plucked turkeys that have had a bad sunburn. These are the bass clarinets, the contrabass clarinets, and the contra-contra-bass clarinets. Most of these instruments play so low that they generally have to cut holes in the floor to let the sound out. They also have saxophones enough for nineteen dance bands, piccolos and clarinets by the gross, and plus all of this, there are always cornets and trumpets and baritones, trombones, and sousaphones galore. The combined wind velocity of whose huffing and puffing is enough to pump up the Graf Zeppelin. Playing a sousaphone is like wrapping a cold python around you and filling its innards with winds of typhoon proportion, only to come out with a sound that is something between a flabby grunt and the bewildered cry of a male moose during the moulting season. I just think it's lucky those things never blow back.

And the whole group uses a "B-flat" to tune to instead of (as in your orchestra) an "A." This is generally given out by the clarinets and everybody starts blowing their instruments with a sort of wishful hope that they are somewhere in the vicinity of it. Having bands tune up sometimes seems about as useless as trying to learn to walk on the water. So, after four or five minutes of febrile honking, all you can do is give up. Wrap vigorously on the side of the metal stand with your metal baton and cry out "from the top!" That's one thing they do teach them in schools—where to start from. And your acres of instruments all start wending their various ways vertically downward where it all ends in one great thud of bass drums and cymbals.

Every year bands get bigger and bigger. But if they don't stop growing, one of these days football fans are going to get crowded right on out of the stadium and they'll be the ones who have to go down on field during half time. The main reasons directors like big bands has nothing to do with music. Band directors are folks who like to spell things, but they use people instead of pencils to do it with. They also like to make things, a sort of humanized Tinkertoy set with built-in music and so every Saturday afternoon they dream up these spectaculars that have everything in them from simulated space shots to the sinking of the Titanic. I was a band director once myself, only in those days we didn't have enough members in the band to spell out long words and so when we played football teams like "Southern Methodist University" or "Texas Agricultural and Mechanical College" we had to use shorthand.

Bands do a lot of dancing on the football field during half-time these days, but I don't think Arthur Murray teaches THEM. Trying to dance if you're wearing a wrap-around Sousaphone or have a bass drum strapped to your stomach is not only a prime example of over-achieved futility, but also terpsichorian awkwardness at its utmost. If I were either a bass horn blower or a drummer I'd find the fellow who invented this kind of football ballet and hang him to the nearest yardline.

But actually, I guess, these things are really not your problem, for you have just come in to "direct" the band at its "practice," not to dance with the snare drummers. Your problems are more profound, actually, like wondering how to co-ordinate this gym full of kids into the limited confines of one or more marches without having your eardrums wrecked beyond any possible repair. There is an old wheeze that makes the rounds every year about why Johnson and Johnson invented Band-Aids. It wasn't so much to cover up minor wounds as it was to give the poor band director something to stuff into his ears until football season was over with.

Sometimes a local symphony conductor will get invited to conduct what is called "band-day" at the stadium and bands come from miles around to participate in this. The object seems to be to see how many thousands of bandsmen you can cram tightly together on the field without inflicting any fatalities from jabbing trombone slides and sharp oboe reeds. The guest "director" stands on something that faintly resembles a launching platform for the Titan III (and no seat belts) and he generally conducts with a baton that's about two yards long with a light on one end. THEY can't follow your beat because your altitude is about 40 feet and their ceiling is zero. When the announcer has finished the countdown, you give them a big strong downbeat and they will all begin—but by the time the trumpets (at the end zone) get to the trio, the drums (on the thirty yard line) will be trying to help the saxophones (on the other thirty) show the sousaphones (in the other end zone) where the place is and presently the whole thing will unwind like a tired LP on a bent turntable. And you're up there, still holding on for dear life, wishing you had remembered to check your insurance and vowing you'll never do it again. But then, a stadium full of screaming spectators applaud your performance like you certainly never heard in *your* concert hall and before you're halfway down to the ground you're already planning a spectacular of your own involving a massed orchestra of giant proportions including a one thousand voice chorus and forty oboes. It does get in your blood!

We have strayed somewhat from our subject (as the King said as he wandered away from the peasant) but we are back now to take up the other names the instruments have besides their English cognomens. Some of them haven't even made it to English yet, such as the *Tympani*. This is freely translated into "kettle drum" or "skin tubs" (as they are referred to by hipsters and that ilk). There are a few other names like "dog house" which is used for the contra bassi (string bass to you), "licorice or gob stick" for clarinet, and the percussion section is often called the "battery' because it sometimes sounds like the Light Brigade has just charged. You should learn a few foreign names like "pauken" for kettle drums *neé* tympani. "Tromboni" is another good one, meaning trombones, of course. If you ever played a piece about Napoleon, for instance, you could say: "Let me see the Napoleon tromboni parts," thus eliciting a merry laugh and much envy at your ready wit.

In Italian, groups of violins are called "violini." It has always struck me as odd that we call the plural of "cello" *"celli"* but that the violins are just called violins. French Horns are called "corni," but use this word sparingly as it is often misinterpreted as a criticism of the *way* they're playing. Study up on this and you'll find some dandy yarns to tell at PTA meetings like about how the English Horn is really French and the French Horn is really English and that the basset horn isn't the one with the long ears, but is actually an almost extinct member of the clarinet family. Stress this "family" bit and your audience will get a great "togetherness" feeling about music, and quote that old one about "put a horn in a boy's hand and he'll never rob a bank." This goes down well, especially if they don't stop to remember that there has never yet been a successful bank robbery with a saxophone or even a fluegalhorn.

There are lots of famous people who played instruments, like George Washington (flute) and Queen Elizabeth the first (virginal) (which was not the reason they called her the Virgin Queen, however). Thomas Paine is supposed to have begun writing his "Age of Reason" on a drumhead until the drummer told him to beat it, and of course, everybody knows that Benjamin Franklin invented the harmonica. He also wrote a string quartet and among his other inventions was the Saturday Evening Post. Work this sort of thing in and then say how universal the arts are with music being the most universal language of all.

A friend of mine thinks garlic is, but he'll have to admit that music is a better background for the universal art of romance than garlic is any day. This universal language bit bugs me sometimes. Some folks think that because a Japanese pianist, a Greek violinist, and a French cellist play a trio by the Austrian Haydn that they are using the universal language to communicate with each other. The true test of this is that they don't play music when they want to know where the men's room is. They get out their handy little pocket translators.

A few paragraphs ago we were talking about interesting sections of the orchestra from the audience's standpoint, and I, for one, like to watch the percussion players, particularly in contemporary music. These guys are triple threat performers and go from tapping on gongs and bells to banging on chimes and beating on tympani and bass drums. Generally a percussion section looks like it was always one man short as they race around like crazy with mallets toward none, and that desperate "we'll never make it" look on their collective faces. I myself write a lot for percussion and have written so much for cowbell that I expect a commission from the National Dairyman's Association in any mail. Ole Bull, the eminent Swedish violinist and composer, was the last one so honored.

Bands go in big for percussion, too, because they are great for drowning out bad intonation and faulty playing. Sometimes it is about all you can hear on TV and radio half-time broadcasts. Except for the glockenspiel, you have to have pretty good ears to hear the tune anywhere else once the drummers get going. The glockenspiel is (or are) bells which are (or is) mounted on a sort of short flagpole which the performer carries against his hipbone or sometimes stomach. They're dangerous, in a way, and surgeons tell me that perforation of the waistline is a nasty repair job. You wouldn't catch me playing one of those things without a tetanus shot first.

Occasionally you will run into a score which calls for electronic instruments. Avoid these if you can as they always take the spotlight away from you. There's one of them particularly where the player weaves his arms around, looking exactly like a tired East Indian snake charmer whose cobra is playing for *him*. It puts out a sound which is not unlike a were-wolf calling to its mate in a whistle factory. Lots of composers use very realistic effects like gunshots in their music. I'm one of these, but I have never yet been allowed real bullets. I remember an early score of Ferde Grofe's called "Tabloid Suite" in which he used everything from fire sirens to typewriters. It was a toss up who would be allowed to play them, firemen and secretaries or union musicians. I would avoid music with guns in it and another kind I would avoid is taped music.

This kind of music is composed (or edited from assorted sounds) directly on tape and not only eliminates the orchestra, but ALSO the conductor. The only important person is the engineer (or the composer who now has become one) as he sits at a tape machine communing with the spirits with a pair of scissors and miles of magnetized tape. Taped composers are those who spend all of their time giving concerts for each other and getting foundation grants.

But even more dangerous to your future is computer music, for it seems like there, they've not only eliminated the conductor and orchestra, but also the audience. Computer music is really enjoyed only by other computers. They get this sound by feeding in a bunch of formulae to a Univac and a couple of hours later, out comes a synthesized symphony. Untouched by human hands. The only trouble with these *avant garde* creators is that they keep insisting that it is music. I can just see it now over at the IBM lab and a couple of Univacs are sitting around during the evening after supper, resting up from computing all day. They're tired, but suddenly one of them starts up again with "3X over nine point two to the hundredth power divided by the square root of the hypotenuse" and the other one lights up, blushing redly in the evening twilight and says:

"Oh darling, you're playing our song."

So when you stand up on that podium and look at the violins (they're the ones UNDER the chin) and at all the other instruments sitting there in their union splendor, let your mind flash back across the years to the time when the great god Pan first heard the wind blow across the reeds and rushes in that swamp—and know that when you give your downbeat, you are setting the centuries in motion. And if you're conducting and do hear some raucous blats out of the brass section, you won't have to say:

"Now who did that?"

You'll know. It was the French Horns—or was it the trombones? Oh well, glare at both of them and maybe next time it *will* be the drummers and then you'll be sure for sure!

CHAPTER X

Way Down Upon The Swami River

This is a chapter, which, if there are small children present, do not read aloud! Also, if any of you have queasy stomachs, vapors, or varicose goosebumps, you'd better not stay either, because it is pretty scary. We are going to discuss a little-known facet of the conductor's art: *Hypnosis.* From the outset, I want to make it clear that hypnotism usually has little or nothing to do with the hips. Its only relationship here is that the musicians will be sitting on that area while you use it on them.

Hypnotism is generally believed to be a state of mind where *your* mind is controlled by somebody else's mind, like in the army or marriage. It is will power, and where there is a will, there is a way. And the way we are telling you about is hypnotism. It is a science that is shrouded in mystery and about the only way to get any information about it is to send twenty-five cents in stamps or coins to this little outfit whose coupon you clip out of the advertising section of some of the types of pulp magazines you run into in barbershops or poolhalls. And they will send you a pamphlet entitled: "You, too, can be a hypnotist!" There is another way to learn about it, but that requires four years of medical school.

Most of you have seen hypnotists work at one time or another, and they are usually fellows who wear turbans and oriental suits and have these sexy girl assistants dressed in flimseys. They get somebody from the audience to come up on stage, and while the orchestra in the pit is playing "Sheik of Araby," this sexy assistant (whom we shall call Chemise La Fer for purposes of our story, but whose real name was Ada Glott), is beckoning to the audience while at the same time doing a series of bumps and grinds which would throw the ordinary spleen out of kilter for months.

The fellow from the audience (now called the "subject") is finally up on the stage and the hypnotist makes a few motions at him with his hands (much like conducting the opening bars of "The Rites of Spring") and mumbles some mumbo-jumbo phrases like "Heavy, heavy hangs over thy head, fine or superfine." He then tells this fellow to go to sleep and sure enough, the subject is asleep. He is now "under," as it is called in the hypnotism trade, except in Australia they call it "down under."

Once he is under, the hypnotist suggests various goofy things for him to do which the subject generally does eagerly. Finally the hypnotist snaps his fingers and gives him a post-hypnotic suggestion to kiss the fat lady in the third row on the way back to his seat—and the subject "returns" (no longer hypnotized), feeling good like he had just dozed off a little (which he could have as easily done back at his seat instead of making a fool of himself on the stage). Chemise La Fer helps him to the footlights and down the ramp, grinding and bumping all the way, and then she runs to the wings to change into her iron girdle as the next act is where she gets sawed in half. Meanwhile, the subject goes on up the aisle, stopping to kiss the fat lady in the third row, and the hypnotist bows so low you wonder how he keeps his turban on.

This is one form of hypnotism, and medical science frowns on it for being charlatanism (it wasn't the charlatan that Ada Glott was dancing, believe you me!), and doctors say it could be dangerous. I frown on it myself, because I once went up on the stage and I'll tell you, kissing fat ladies in the third row is not my idea of entertainment.

But hypnosis is not one of the black arts like witchcraft, sorcery, or commercials, and it has been practiced by such allied arts as politics and religion for years. Who among you has not heard of the old time orators who could put a spell over the audience? Here lately, dentistry has been taking it up somewhat, and I may say in passing that I wish to hell my own dentist knew something about it. But either he is a sadist or against progress. The only relation it has to dentistry so far, is the old Mosaic dictum of "an eye for an eye and a tooth for a tooth," which brings up the subject of eyes and their use in hypnosis. I really didn't mean to bring up teeth at all.

The eyes are known in the medical game as the "myopic muscles" or sometimes "orbs." Orbital flight is something different and we don't have space to discuss it right now. The eyes are (and here I quote directly from the King James, or the Revised Version of Grey's Anatomy) "what you look out of and are to be found on either side of the nose, right under the eyebrows." I think Grey put that rather nicely.

It is customarily believed that the eyes are the vital factor in hypnosis, but we shall see that it depends on several other factors including (though not necessarily restricted to) the lymph glands, osmosis, and an old copy of Norman Vincent Peale's "The Power of Positive Thinking," which is about to be made into a movie called "The Thinking of Positive Power," a documentary about the TVA.

Hypnosis is done through a process called "suggestion," and before you start thinking that this whole idea is rather suggestive, let me say that: if you keep suggesting to yourself "I think I can, I think I can, I think I can," well, hell you can. Especially if you are a little train. This is called self-hypnosis or auto-suggestion (not to be confused with General Motors' sales campaigns). There was a branch of this stuff called "Mesmerism," but it didn't catch on too well. However, one Monsieur Coué (a Frenchman) had a vogue for awhile with his "every day in every way, I get better and better and better" before the doctors stamped it out as it was cutting down on their office calls. Doctors are also against the apple business, come to think of it.

We could go pretty deeply into this business of hypnotism (I sent away my twenty-five cents, remember?), but we actually won't talk about any part of it except as it directly relates to the sort of mating trance that goes on between conductor and his collective "subject," the orchestra. Rule one is: it is easier for you to impose your will over them than it is for them to gang up on you and get you to do what they want you to do! They don't need hypnotism for that anyway, they've got a union! So you are safe from them, but they aren't even half-safe from you once you decide to give them the old eye that binds them immutably to your every whim and desire. If they even look up, they're lost. But if they lose their place in the music while they're looking up, then YOU'RE lost. That's the only real danger in hypnosis, unless of course, you have had the foresight also to hypnotize the audience not to notice if anything goes wrong.

Hypnosis for the conductor requires only a few simple tools. The podium is the most important one, and it is symbolic of your power. Stand beside it and you are a pigmy, but stand upon it and you are king-sized, and—if you will it so—in complete control by virtue of just being there. It's like a preacher's pulpit. A preacher gets up and says: "We will now all stand and sing number 328." And they all do. In all of my years of going to church, I have never heard anybody sing anything except what they were told to sing. And stand up while doing it, too. And anyone who has ever sat through a long sermon on a hot July day will recall immediately the hypnotic spell of the voice that drones you right on into peaceful sleep. They really ought to take up the collection during that time instead of before you are fully under and can think for yourself.

The podium is the same type of symbol and the first time I became aware of it was one day when I got up on one to change a light bulb in the band room of a friend of mine. No sooner had I gotten up there than this room full of tootling youngsters got very quiet and they looked up at me hopefully as if they were wishing I would command them to do something. I couldn't think of anything at the time, but afterwards I was so impressed by my discovery that I tried to get a copyright on it. My letter was evidently sent to the Pentagon by mistake and it's been classified material ever since. Until now, at least.

I would say then, that the first step to a practical use of hypnosis in conducting is the step you take up to the podium itself. You have prepared the subjects, as it were, and are now ready to put them a little more soundly under your spell. Start talking at once about nothing in particular while at the same time turning the pages of your score furiously, but first look at them for a minute and say simply:

"Tschaikowsky!"

And if somebody doesn't say "Gesundheit," you know that you've pronounced it right. Now notice that you don't say "Tschaikowsky's 4th Symphony, 2nd movement." Just "Tschaikowsky!"

Immediately they all start looking through their music and get it out ready to play. Out of all the music that Tschaikowsky wrote, you have (with one simple statement—through telepathy and through thought-transference) excited their extrasensory perception to the point that they KNOW exactly WHICH Tschaikowsky you're talking about. The fact that there's only one Tschaikowsky piece on their stands has nothing to do with it. It's almost as if you KNEW it was the only one they had and unerringly called it out, and they will marvel, yea, even quaver and quake with fear.

But don't let them start playing yet. Riffle through your score pages and let them wait anxiously for a minute or so. They don't know what you want yet. They only (individually) hope that whatever it is, it won't concern them personally—especially to the point where they have to play something by themselves.

Say something like: "Seven bars before letter 'O' in the 2nd movement." Then you wait until they all riffle *their* pages. This sound is not unlike the quiet shuffling of playing cards during a lonely Solitaire game and has a soothing effect, preparing them for more euphoria. When they have all found letter "O," suddenly bark out sternly:

"French Horns, six measures after letter 'K.' Let's hear it!" Give a quick downbeat and chances are that at least two of them will miss it, either that or knock out a tooth or so in the all-out effort. This gives you a chance to say:

"I said the SIXTH bar. One two three four five six." They all count up to six carefully and you say:

"Well, *are* you or are you *not* ready?"

Before they have a chance to answer, turn to the violins and talk over something with them and so on through the orchestra. You are getting them all into a state of "readiness" to respond to your INSTANT WISH (a product of the Aladdin Company), and very soon you'll have them all ready for phase three, which is called "group submission."

"Da Capo!" you say, but you don't say it very loudly so that some of them won't hear it and have to ask you what you said. This puts them in a state of dependence and they are so anxious to help that they almost plead with you to repeat what you said. Say it louder next time, but look hurt and pretend your work gets harder every day.

Then raise your hands. Notice that automatically they will all raise up their instruments, ready to await your command. Even some of those who don't even have any notes to play will snap into what we hypnotic scientists call the "playing posture," however, they will grin foolishly and sheepishly put them back down again when they realize what they've done. Don't make the mistake of giving the downbeat immediately, though. Look slowly around the orchestra searchingly as if you were peering into their very souls and cower them a little more. Then drop your arms in a sort of futile gesture and say: "Let me hear an 'A.' "

You have accomplished two hypnotic gestures in a single stroke here. You have prevented them from playing (which put them in a mood of deep fear that you won't let them show you how good they are), and you've got them all worried about their "A." In short, you've diverted their attention from the whole collection of notes it takes to make up a Tschaikowsky Symphony, to just one single note, their tuning note "A." The concert master will jump up and point at the oboe and he will sound out the "A" and then the whole orchestra will become a frenzy of blowing and bowing as they frantically search for the missing "A." Sir Arthur Sullivan didn't have that much trouble finding the whole lost chord.

You listen to them for a few seconds and tap sharply on the concert master's stand and say:

"Well, finally!"

This also accomplishes two things. It not only subdues them into a state of wanting to play again, but the concert master scrambles back to his seat to avoid being lacerated by your twitching baton. Keep him at bay at all times, as he sits dangerously close to the podium and has probably been taking a correspondence course in conducting secretly now for seven years.

Now you are ready for the final step. Lift your hands high again and give them a downbeat. They are now in your power, fully hypnotized. Respect this power highly. Tremble before it, because you have made their wills subject to your own. In musical hypnosis it is dangerous to go any further than this, as they could start regressing —which is a state of living momentarily in previous times and they're liable to start making fonky noises like they did when they were taking music lessons. If this accidentally happens, stop the orchestra at once and talk directly to the regressed player. Say something like:

"By the way, did you know that wonderful first chair flute of the Denver Symphony? I heard he was leaving there and looking for a job." Now there is nothing that will snap a performer out of anything, much less hypnosis, than to hear that there is another man available for his job. This is known medically as the Stokes-Cheyne respiratory effect of "holding your breath for fear it will be me the next time he picks on somebody" procedure.

Of all the members of the orchestra, the bass drummer and the tympanist are the hardest to hypnotize. First of all, they have a harder time lifting up their instruments at the "ready" signal, and besides that, they are armed more lethally than you are. They are also accustomed to beating the hell out of things. With a tympanist, you can always use that old "you're out of tune" routine, and keep him cranking those heads up and down while saying "flat" and "sharp" at him. Tympani players never oil their tuning rods and it always sounds a little like a rusty oxcart axle or letting down the drawbridge when they tune up. They're always and forever putting their ears right on top of the drum heads, too, pretending to be tuning them, while in reality they've got a small radio in there and are listening to the ball game or the racing results. As for bass drummers, they generally don't like music anyway or else why should they take up bass drum? So in the case of these two fellows, it is sometimes better to fraternize than hypnotize. A friendly little game of pinochle or casino occasionally (in which you lose) will keep them on your side and they won't want to lose you as their conductor ever, as nobody likes to lose a steady source of extra income.

With a little practice, you can put your orchestra (except for those two) in a state of hypnosis quickly and keep them that way. If they start getting restless, you can always use stronger dosages, some of which you can pick up by watching animal trainers work. This is apt to backfire dangerously, however, as I remember hearing of one conductor that got rather carried away after a refresher course at Barnum and Bailey's even to the point of wearing whipcord pants and a pith helmet to rehearsals, and one day was severely bitten in the shanks by an English Horn player who thought he was a Bengal Tiger. This required seven stitches and buffet suppers for the conductor for months and he never did get to show anybody his scar. So don't use these drastic methods if you can help it, for your musicians just might look up at you as through those bars and go amok!

Trombone players are pretty hard to hypnotize, too, as they are always ducking down behind their music stands under the pretext of letting the spit out of their horns or oiling their slides. Besides, they've got a pretty magical looking act themselves, as over two-thirds of the audience still believe that they swallow those slides—which is more than you can do with your baton! You may have to use extreme measures with them and give them a little pre-rehearsal seance at which you use the famous Irish hypnotist's technique, referred to in the trade as "O'Flattery." Come to think of it, they really don't swallow those slides, *do they?*

In your practice of these various techniques, don't ever stand in front of a mirror and watch yourself. A friend of mine did that and hypnotized himself so severely that he started regressing and was last seen in the 18th century walking backward toward Leipzig to visit Johann Sebastian Bach.

Don't forget the audience in your hypnotic planning, for they are easy subjects. In fact, they are already partly hypnotized by social pressures which make it incumbent upon them to be seen at symphony concerts if they are to be considered cultured or, if they have a mink coat. They are pre-conditioned to do things like applaud when you come out on stage (and why should they, really, because you haven't done anything but walk out there?). This is a form of hypnosis which they can work on you actually, for by the simple gesture of beating their palms together, they can keep you walking out from the wings and bowing as long as they want to keep it up. Unless you stop them, that is, and you should exercise this form of counter-control just to prove you have the final say. Raise your hand in a sort of gesture meaning "Please, folks, I am not really worthy of all this" and then when they quiet down, use of O'Flattery technique on them with "You are the best audience yet." And then they'll not only applaud *you* for saying so, but also applaud *themselves* for being, and they'll leave the hall so happy about the whole thing that they won't remember that horrible moment when you cued in the clarinets and the trombones came in instead.

Lots of times you can use hypnosis on an audience by getting them to do what is sometimes called "community singing." This is always great around Christmas, and the average symphony goer will sing up a storm on "Silent Night" if you will just conduct him at it. You wave your arms hypnotically and even a man who wouldn't be caught dead singing in the shower will bellow out on a Christmas carol like he was a re-constituted Enrico Caruso. This is great stuff for your mass hypnosis practice, but it sure must cause consternation around the throne of God when a whole hall-full of people are trying to sound like a Herald Angel singing "Hark."

Not too much of this type of audience hypnosis, though, or they'll want to sing at every concert and the first thing you know, you'll end up having to schedule things like "Sing along with Guiseppi Verdi" nights.

The biggest challenge to your powers as a hypnotist and the greatest value of its knowledge (outside of the orchestra and the audience, that is) concerns the Board of Directors. These are the guys who can sign your renewal contract and so try to keep *them* in a semi-comatose state at all times. The O'Flattery technique is okay here, but you must induce it in reverse and have *them* O'Flatter *you.* Hold small and intimate dinner parties with candles, incense, and plenty of shiny reflection surfaces. In case you're not completely sure of yourself, I'd suggest that the reflection surfaces be things like extra-strong Manhattans, wine with dinner, and large brandies afterwards.

The technique you're using here is the Schiklegruber (or divide and conquer) method. Suggest gently (the flickering candle light plus three Manhattans will give your eyes *such* a Svengali look) that you regard their opinions highly and your respect for them is nothing short of profound. "And" (you can say while adjusting any reflecting surface such as a highly polished cherry in a Manhattan glass) "I do agree with your suggestion that new blood be brought in." (Meaning "theirs," not "yours." . . .) And here you let your voice trail away into the distance, inferring that you simply cannot bring yourself to say that *some* of them want *some others of them* off the board entirely. They will not only follow you, they will be way ahead of you, because all of them have a friend they'd rather have on the board than . . . (and here their voices trail off into the distance). This sort of hypnotism is dangerous, for it has "delayed" reaction and should never be used unless you have taken the Hypocritical Oath. In the meantime, while they're churning around, all individually hoping to become the new Symphony President, you can get your contract signed by individually promising each of them that you will support them in getting their friends on the Board. And—if the Manhattans were really good—you may even get a raise.

As far as we know, this is the first time in the history of either magic, medicine, or music that this subject has been so frankly discussed as a necessary part of the total equipment for a conductor. No doubt it will soon be introduced into the music schools as a standard course right along with the treble clef and such. And it's about time, too, for it sure works—and because *it* does, *you* can. Only one thing, though. No conductor will ever dare to look another conductor straight in the eye for fear of being turned back into a second violinist again.

Study it well, for next to voodoo and TV, it's the best thing that's come along since social security. All of us composers have known about it for years.

How else do you think we've gotten our music played?

If you have to go, put them on their honor—either that or take it with you.

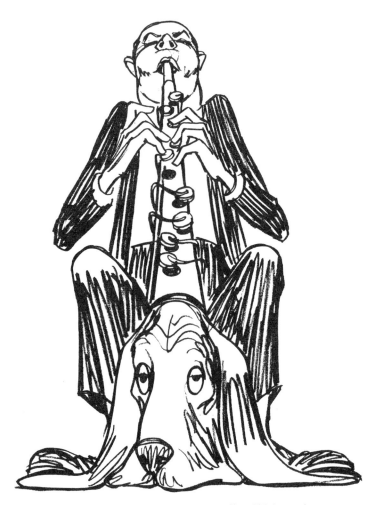

There are some dandy yarns you can tell at PTA meetings—.

Chapter XI

Intermission—Ten Minutes

I just happen to be a world-shaking authority on intermissions, and although I do not list this fact in my autobiography because there are just some things you don't brag about, I have intermished with the best of them in some of the greatest concert halls both here and abroad (Ah, abroad!). I would not be saying these things unless they were true, and also unless I was leading up to what is one of the most important (and until now, little talked-about) parts of a conductor's career—the intermission.

And it concerns you (the conductor) in your dressing room, and them (the public) out in the lobby, and no matter how versed you are in the magic, myths, and marvels of music, you are lost unless you know all about these all-important ten minutes!

Intermissions are always risky for a conductor, because it is the first chance the audience has to get out from under his spell. If he could only mingle with them, it might all be different. But he can't because he is in his dressing room and we'll talk about that sacred area later. One thing about this book, if there's anything we don't try to be helpful about, I don't know what it is.

For some people, intermissions are the most popular parts of concerts, for it allows them (along with several hundred other people) to jam into a foyer that's even too small for forty, and to blow cigarette smoke in each other's faces while giving out unsolicited opinions about the concert. It is a time when reputations may be shredded like so much confetti as each ticket-holder tries to impress all of the others (at the top of his voice) with how much he knows about what is going on. For the most part, this is rather harmless fun for them as it gives them a chance to use their big musical words and nod knowingly about the performance as if each had studied the score for hours before coming to the concert. Large-bosomed ladies joust for position so they can stand near one or more of the critics to hear what they're talking about or to shriek out some *bon mot* at them in the hopes that they'll be quoted in the morning Gazette. Little do they know that the first thing a music critic does during intermission is to turn off his hearing-aid.

Ex-opera singers, identifying their own careers with those of the reigning Maestro, go around quoting like "And my dear, he's simply marvelous with Carmen" even though the nearest the conductor has ever gotten to Carmen so far was one whose last name was "Cavallero" who once played at his college prom. Those ex-opera singers are ubiquitous. If they have sons, they are called sons of ubiquitous. This word means "always around" and if you know ex-opera singers like I do, they are always around 195 pounds in their stocking feet and teach singing locally at the conservatory. But they are always your friends, especially if they have already retired and if you don't hire any of their ex-rivals to appear with you, they'll deck the halls with boughs of laurel in your behalf as they go on and on about how terrific you are, loudly predicting that you're headed for the Met or at least La Scala. If there aren't any in your town, I wouldn't hesitate to hire one just to have at concerts for intermission propagandizing. A sort of a "yakkity clacque" as it were. I will say no more of these ladies except that generally their first name is Madam.

Another of the lady creatures that is apt to be swirling around in the undulating mob of restroom-hunters and opinion-givers is the lady conductor. Ladies have a hard time conducting, but many of them feel the call and seldom, if ever, stop trying. Generally this provokes gentle merriment from witty critics, one of whom wrote (as I recall it) "Her Mozart and Tschaikowsky are pretty terrible, but I understand her biscuits are divine!" No matter how they dress for a concert, they just don't seem to come out well when viewed from the south while they are conducting north.

However, there will always be one (or more) in your town and you can keep her (or them) happy by suggesting that one of these days you're going on a vacation and you'll be looking for a temporary replacement. Hold this out as an ever-dangling bait and you'll have a constant friend for intermission chit-chat about how great you are. You'll recognize the lady conductor easily, because she'll always have scores under her arm and generally a bag of what looks to be knitting, but is in reality batons instead of needles.

As viewed from above, there seems to be perpetual motion in the foyer, not unlike the mating dance of the pelican except not as productive, for pelicans *do* produce other pelicans. The crowd surges to-and-fro, greeting its most mortal enemy as "darling" and asking each other if they knew that Jan Peerce or Van Cliburn was in the audience and that they were thrilled to death because they just had an intimate little chat with him (or them). This sets everybody in motion counter-clockwise looking for the celebrities, all the while puffing more cigarettes as if smoking was going to be outlawed any minute. Some of the older ones, remembering the Volstead Act, smoke two at a time.

Young matrons rush to telephones to instruct their baby sitters on the ten o'clock feeding, (rule: if it is too hot for the kid to drink, then it's too hot to test on your wrist) and young matrons' husbands phone up the local newspaper to find out how the basketball game is going which is where they would rather be going than where they went. And through it all is this constant hubba-hubba of voices that reminds you of the Tower of Babel on opening day. The natives are restless for sure, but mainly because they're afraid the intermission will end before they've had a chance to impress their quota and get to use words like "mixo-lydian," "bubonic," and "dodecaphonic." This latter words refers to the twelve-tone school of writing, or "dodecafanatic" group.

So they push and pull and shove and surge and circumnavigate the hall until the signal bell rings and then, as if by magic, they begin their re-entry procedure—the study of which by the National Space Agency gained them all sorts of knowledge leading to our own conquest of the upper regions. And they are happy because they have had their fun smoking at each other and going to the Men's Room (as the case may be) and proclaiming their own volumned-views about music —positive that they have impressed everybody within earshot and will shortly be invited to lecture before the Music Guild. They are thoroughly rejuvenated and ready now for the final portion of their culture as they worship at the shrine of music with you (their conductor) as high priest. Even the music critics turn their hearing aids back up. At least a little.

Meanwhile, back in the dressing room, you are still great (no matter what some son-of-a-ubiquitous critic might say later). You have stepped off of the stage following your curtain calls and go into your little sanctum-sanctorum smelling vaguely like a pole-vaulter or a basketball gym and so you will need a minute to freshen up before you begin granting your audiences to the privileged. A little Air-Wick will do wonders for you, but a standard brand cologne will help you even more. The never-ending battle between a conductor and his sweat glands is a subject fit for a full-length book in itself. But we won't tell all here. Mum is the word.

Intermission for conductors may be divided roughly into three categories: (a) receiving the VIP's, (b) last minute instructions to (or from) guest soloists, and (c) intermission broadcasts. We will skip (b) entirely as such sessions are top secret and also uninteresting to the general public. After all, just what could be interesting about a guest soloist beseeching and pleading with the conductor to let him at least finish the cadenza before he starts in conducting the coda?

First, then, we will take up the "parade of the privileged." There are some people who don't really give a damn about music, but who just can't resist going backstage during an intermission to see the conductor. This is the same crowd that goes to watch boxers bleed after a twelve-round bout. And they go there because there is a certain status symbol about getting into dressing rooms *during* intermissions when the general public has to wait until the concert is over. They like to tell about it later with stuff like: "Last night at intermis-

Computer music is really enjoyed only by other computers.

You are getting them all into a state of "readiness"—.

sion, Maestro Glop was really fatigued, poor dear. You know how generally his veins just stand out on his forehead? Well last night they were just lying there. If he doesn't give up Brahms, he may not live through the season!" Note how this also indicates a vast knowledge of medicine with this instant diagnosis.

Actually Brahms isn't a fatal disease at all, although for some people it does provoke a certain drowsiness somewhat akin to sleeping sickness. Or they will say stuff like: "I've never seen Maestro happier with his orchestra." What they don't realize is that you are happy because you've GOT an orchestra. This group are always great gushers and if we could get them all together, we wouldn't have to depend on the Mid-East for oil.

Sometimes there is a sort of sneaky one among them who will come out with "Maestro, *never* have I heard a Brahms like that!" This can be interpreted variously as (a) she has never heard any Brahms before and doesn't want to say so, (b) she has your Brahms mixed up with a Sam Brahms that wrote a no-hitter pop tune called "I would like to be with you" in A-flat, or (c) she is casting aspersions on your own Brahms as compared to some other conductor's Brahms. But in any event, interpret her meaning to your advantage (as if there could be a better Brahms-beater than you, well really!) and blush prettily and take the whole thing with a grain of salt. Or maybe two grains of aspirin is a better recipe.

The worst kind of a privileged intermission visitor is a club woman who has a protege pianist in tow. The object of her visit is to get you interested in presenting this gifted little monster at some future youth concert and you have to let her in because her club sold the most tickets to the Symphony Ball. She's got rocks, not only in her head, but in four banks in town—all of which her husband is Chairman of the board of. He's not with her because he goes bowling on concert nights. One of the special privileges of the very rich is "not going" to concerts. Just because they happen to help defray the annual deficit for tax purposes, is no sign they have to go. And there are always deficits just as there are always tax purposes.

The protege who is with her already has two concerti under his belt as well as a duodenal ulcer and couldn't care less about the autograph which you so graciously give him, as he knows that the trade value with the other kids is ten of yours for one of Hugh Downs or two of Fidel Castro's.

The other type of intermission event is the busy, busy radio intermission-type interview over the local station that uses your concert as an FCC pacifier to keep from getting its license revoked for broadcasting nothing but Rock and Roll interspersed with beer commercials. The announcer is generally one of those fellows who can't say "fugue" without coaching, either that or a guy who has read Milton Cross's stuff on music and still doesn't know who got the girl in Aida. His companion is a foggy-eyed engineer who squints at a bunch of flickering dials and keeps saying "testing woof, testing woof." Some day one of these guys is going to cry "woof" once too often. His attitude toward symphony music is neutral and nothing ever bothers him except when the tympani plays too loud—and it always does if there is a microphone around. The whole set-up has been scotch-taped together and fixed with bailing wire so there's always a danger of a short circuit with resultant 5th or 6th degree burns if you're not careful. The interview generally begins with the announcer saying in his best "I speak to you from Mount Olympus" style.

"We are broadcasting to you from the sweat-drenched dressing room of Maestro Sylvester Glop, the dynamic director of our local sympathy orchestra. And tonight this interview is being dedicated to Bill and Mary, Slim and Esther, Sally and Pete, Lum and Abner, and Death and Transfiguration—the latter number which is being featured this week at Hearse's Funeral Home, the Mortuary with the Friendly Lay-away plan. And now, Maestro (and he always pronounces "Maestro" as if it were "Mice-tro"), how do you think things have gone out there tonight so far?"

He says this as if he thought the whole thing needed embalming. You respond almost gaily, considering that your sponsor is Hearse's "Rent-A-Casket."

"Well, uh, I felt that the orchestra rose to supreme heights, especially in the passacaglia where the oboe has the mordent."

"Oh!" he says, completely baffled with words like "passacaglia" and "mordent" which is why you said them to baffle him with. Actually you also baffled Bill and Mary, Slim and Esther, Sally and Pete, and all those other folks out there in friendly radio land, too. The announcer recovers quickly (no dead air now, even if we are sponsored by a funeral home).

"Tell me" he says, telling you to tell him and at the same time reading a question he has written on the back of an old envelope in the hopes that it will become as immortal as the Gettysburg address, "is it true that Handel wrote the Messiah in 21 days?"

This is the kind of a question which makes you want to say "Yes, but he didn't get an answer" but you don't dare quip because a lot of your best subscribers are pillars of the church, and besides, don't forget that minister on your board of directors. You can launch into a four or five-minute answer on this or on Odo of Cluny or Hucbald the Elder or any other damn thing that comes to your mind, as he is not listening anyway. What he is doing is checking his stopwatch to see how the time is holding out and also trying to think up another question in case it is. Finally he breaks in on you with:

"What are your plans once the season is over, Mice-tro?" and you (remembering your refresher course in Rand-McNally) start talking about Paris (ah, Paris!), Rome, Secaucas, and after that, two weeks in Bali. And he thinks you're talking about "ballet" and the whole thing ends up in such confusion that even Milton Cross would have committed hari-kari, whether he could have pronounced it or not.

The interview closes with an invitation for the audience to listen to the rest of the concert and also to be buried by Hearse's Funeral Home. And the radio crew departs, leaving you barely enough time to sneak a strong blast at a handy vodka crock before you flail away at the last half of the program which is called in the trade: "The Prelude to the Exodus."

We didn't discuss costumes to wear during intermissions. Just don't get too gaudy about it. Intermissions are more than just a time when you get a chance to change your shirt, double-check your collar sprocket, tighten your garters, and take one last quick look in the double full-length mirrors to see if your tails are even. It is a time when announcers won't stop talking and the lobby crowd has had its own fling at self-expression and when the privileged come back to see you in your solitude—and it's bothersome. But if it didn't happen at all, you'd worry why it didn't. It's vital to your career, this swiftly-moving time backstage called "Intermission—Ten Minutes."

Ten minutes, hell! It seems more like a century. And so, your loins all girded, you wend your way back with one triumphant "all eyes open, here I come" and acknowledge their applause with seeming modesty as you leap upon your throne of thrones to set the centuries into motion once again with zest, enthusiasm, and gusto, hoping against hope that your shirt sleeves won't come on down over your fingers, the only thing you forgot to check before you came on stage.

And out in the lobby with the din of *"Symphony No. 5½"* or some such masterpiece as background music, the custodian is looking at the butt-covered floor disgustedly.

"Oh, well" he sighs, "At least the dadblamed idiots don't chaw!"

*Two-thirds of audience believe that trombone players
swallow those slides.*

*For some people, intermissions are the most popular parts
of concerts—.*

CHAPTER XII

Hi Fi, Ho Hum

"How high is Fi?" asked Alice.
"What kind of talk is that?" demanded the March Hare, "especially from a little girl?"
"It's no stranger than you asking me if Pi are square!" said Alice.
"Oh, dear" said the Dormouse, looking at his watch and chain. "It's half after already."
"Half after what?" asked Alice.
"Time" he replied, "and it's a pity, too. We're almost out of it."

The foregoing is a modified quotation from a book I once read and I use it here as a springboard into the subject that I want to take up next which is all about Hi-Fi and why you—as a candidate for conducting honors should not only be aware of it, but know about it as completely and thoroughly as I do.

How conductors ever made it before the invention of the phonograph record is beyond me. Or maybe they didn't and just said they did since there aren't any recordings available of their performances to check up on them. Anyway, now that they are here with the Fi so Hi that you can get a nosebleed just from turning on your set, it's up to you to behoove yourself into getting fully cognizant on the subject and besides that, you should know as much as possible. For you, the King of Music in your town, the throne is being tottered and your whole domain in danger from this malevolent menace of the home style super-juke box. For the nonce we'll set out along the path of learning and if you can't learn it all, you can at least pick up the patter that makes you seem as if you know your stuff. As we have pointed out before, jargonese plus a nimble wit can fool all of the people all of the time no matter what Abe Lincoln said. If indeed he really did say it at all.

The phonograph (as you will recall from remembering them) is a gadget which, if you put a record on it and drop the needle into the groove, you will hear music come out of the speaker. The phonograph is not new (unless you've just gotten one of the latest models) and I believe if memory hasn't failed me, that the first record of recorded speech came when somebody said "What miracles hath God wrought" into it. Or that may have been the telephone. Anyway phonography dates back a good many years and when it first started it was such a miracle that you didn't care what something sounded like because the fact that it sounded at all was enough to have your neighbors in just to show them. It was then a simple, uncomplicated world and if you wanted to hear a recording you cranked it up, lifted the lid, put the needle on, and that was that.

Progress, however, has got the best of this industry like everything else and to properly accommodate yourself to the equipment now available, one should really first take four years at M.I.T. or at least have an electronics engineer as a close friend or bosom companion. Gone are the days when you whittled out your own needle from a cactus bush or rosebranch. It is not so simple anymore and because it isn't, here I am again to teach you the terms that will qualify you as—if not an expert—an "afficianado" or at least a "buff." So from pre-amp to microgroove, from cathode follower to sonic radiation (I just made that last one up), you'll be able to talk glibly about it all, including pick-ups (non-liquid), tone arms, transistors, and stereo. Especially stereo because that's the big thing and it simply means that two speakers (formerly one) will put out the music of the right side of the orchestra from the right speaker, while the music from the left side of the orchestra comes out of the left speaker. What happens to the guys in the middle of the orchestra is as yet unexplained.

"One can" (according to a recent blurb written by one of the bards of Madison Avenue) "close one's eyes with stereo and see the orchestra with one's ears," all of which is about the neatest trick of the week and it conjures up a pretty picture of reversing the idea and stopping up your ears to hear it with your eyes. Or stopping up your nose and not being able to smell something which smells all for the world like a hunk of advertising copy.

You have to learn about this kind of stuff to be able to help stamp out same, because I'll explain later in a paragraph as yet unwritten, how it is now either YOU or STEREO. And personally I'm hoping it's you because composers need conductors more than gadgets.

First of all, get yourself a bunch of back issues of all the audio and fidelity magazines. I suggest back issues because this stuff changes so quickly that you won't know what you want for yourself until you can see what you would have had but wouldn't want now if you had gotten it earlier. For some reason or other my suggestion about the back issues reminds me that when I was in the National Geographic Office recently to get my subscription filled, I noticed that *their* waiting room was filled with a bunch of old Medical magazines.

So out of all of the components (a technical word for gadgets such as amplifiers, tone arms, etc.) you have now selected the very best that money can buy. And by cashing in a few war bonds and selling your mother, you go into the Hi-Fi Center and the first thing he does is try to sell you a kit.

A kit, in the parlance of the trade, is a bundle of wires and a bunch of tubes which you are supposed to hook up yourself according to a schematic written by the same fellow who wrote the lyrics for income tax forms, and so don't do it. It's the same principle as if you wanted to buy a new car and they wanted to sell it to you a wheel at a time. Ignoring your chance to have done it yourself, buy what you think you'll need (until the next issue comes out at least) and then make sure that they guarantee to install it, for next to finding the money to pay for a hi-fi system, putting it together once you get it is your biggest problem. But let's say it's installed and every unit is lit up like a Macy's Christmas tree and your walls are lined with shelves filled with all of the latest releases, and you boost the gain and fill the room (and the house and the neighborhood) with music. You are now a part of the human race which has, in these enlightened days, traded in the birthright that is music for the mess that is pottage (if you'll excuse this out-of-phase metaphor).

None the less, as I keep saying, since you're the symphony conductor, you've got to be Mister Big in your town in *all* matters musical, live or microgrooved. Your tape machine has to be the ampexyish, your amplifiers must be the fireyish, and your whole system should be such a galaxy that all who see it are stricken with awe and wonderment. But you know, gentle student, not even this is enough.

For besides all of this, you have to be a collector. Not just any old collector with stuff like Beethoven's 9th and such. Even if you owned all the editions of Beethoven's 9th (no small feat if you'll consult the Schwann listings), even that isn't sufficient. For the paradox of our times is that, although your equipment has to be the latest thing out—in order for you to be considered an *expert* expert, you have to possess a bunch of collector's items, and the scratchier and older the records are, the better. A sort of disc-coverer, as it were!

So you set yourself up as a collector and in this case we're going to imagine that you're creatively imaginative enough to hit the jackpot by having found the complete recordings (or as it is sometimes called, "discography") and you have found not only the complete set, but the ONLY set of discs ever made by Thelma Slurg, the seconda donna of the Uberhaven Schlottshaus Opera who sang minor roles in the last of the last century. Now lucky for you, Madame Slurb just happened to be around when the fellows from the Edison Company were in town and she was available to render up a few arias—the only seven she knew, as a matter of fact. And now they are preserved for all time on some cylindrical wax recordings that are so fragile they would crumble if you even looked at them. And had you not (at great expense) had them transferred to tape, they would be forever lost.

The fact that when you play the tapes it sounds like a banshee wailing in a hailstorm has nothing whatsoever to do with the value of these acquisitions. What *is* valuable about them is that (a) they are the only ones like them in the world (Madame Slurg was assassinated by an arch-duke named Serbia just before World War I), and (b) they were discovered in the loft of an old log cabin just outside of Grawn, Michigan which in itself is a nice story because, if you think recordings this rare are hard to find, you ought to try looking for Grawn, Michigan! And besides this, (c) you've got them!

And so when your friends come over to get high on Fi, you can wave the latest recordings and tapes aside with a lofty flick of your emerald cuff-links and say:

"But wait until you hear this!"

And with half-veiled eyes and faces all aglow, they'll listen to Madame Slurg and they won't dare not like it because you've got the only ones in the world—a factor which not only gives you fame and prestige, but all the rights and privileges thereunto attached (as they say on diplomas).

You'll be up to your kilocycles in adulation and if you really work it right, you can get a kickback from the local Hi-Fi Center as your friends rush madly from your house to buy a system of their own, complete with some scratchy records of the Gilhooley Concert Band made in Dublin two years before the phonograph was actually invented.

You could laugh at all of this (for there is a bit of humor skulking around the edge of this chapter) except that—Mr. Would-be-Conductor, it would be like laughing at your own funeral with the joke undeniably on you. Let me elucidate.

Somehow in our generation the public has music all mixed up with Hi-Fi sound. Hi-Fi is, you know, short for High Fidelity—a phrase in which the last word means "faithful" and the first describes the prices they charge you for it. And a generation-worth of high pressure advertising and a lot of low resistance has created a condition where the average hi-fi fan isn't concerned with *how* you conduct Beethoven, but how does it sound on his system! And gradually their tastes have turned toward those composers and compositions whose music shows off their equipment best. And their comments go:

"Beethoven can't compare with Bulichoff in the upper end of the sound spectrum, but I'll take Bach over Buxtehude any day when it comes to lows."

After all (they reason) why play a piece that demands only part of their system's capability? No point in short-changing their ears with middle-range music. Now most of these jokers can't hear anything at all above 8,000 cycles if they are over thirty years old, but the equipment they buy goes all the way up to 30,000 cycles. No wonder there are so many dog psychiatrists these days. Those high frequencies are driving the little beasties plumb out of their skulls.

I've had people ask me to come over to hear their equipment (never their recordings or tapes, always their "equipment") with the same reverent gleam once reserved for viewing the Mona Lisa. Once I went to hear a brand new set that a friend of mine had flung together in a financial frenzy that would have awe-stricken Diamond Jim Brady, and when I sat down, he turned the set on with maximum decibels and shouted over the roar of a dirty party record:

"This stereo sure beats the hell out of mono-rail!" And then we listened to records that showed off his highs, to tapes that proved that his woofer and tweeter were woofing and tweeting correctly, and we heard discs that demonstrated that HIS lows were about as low as you could go without squatting down.

The thing that got me is that we didn't listen to any piece all the way through. We just heard those parts that justified all of the money he had spent on what I call "ear-gear." And my friend isn't some singularly remote eccentric. He's a proto-type of the breed that's developed who know more about sonics than sonatas, milligrams than Mendelssohn, and more of filters than fugues. One fellow told me about his "hysteresis" synchronization with a pride normally reserved for winning the Pulitzer Prize or rising from the dead.

In short, this stereo-typed audiophile is a real threat to you and your podium. For something has convinced him that the only difference between your form of music making and his is that yours just isn't in the groove. And since he can play louder than you can, add highs and lows at will, fiddle with your acoustics, and besides that—turn you off, why does he need you?

One critic even wrote a book explaining not only how to listen to music, but how to listen to it as *he* thinks it should be heard on what *he* thinks is the perfect hi-fi, and to hell with what the conductor had in mind when he recorded it. And his pages are filled with the exact settings of the gadgets that control highs and lows and how to get the proper treble turnover and the correct bass response. If he could find a machine that had a knob on it for changing the conductor's tempi (or maybe even the conductor himself), I think he'd enjoy that facility, too.

It probably seems to you that I'm up on a soap box shouting at the top of my voice when in reality I'm standing on a converted speaker chassis with the grill cloth off, the better to amplify the sound of my own voice as I warn the world of batoneering that a "little bug" is going to get you someday! And that little bug's name is HI-FI unless you get it first. Instead of systems that are converted to stereo, our job is to convert the listener back to music that is living because it *is* music and not merely a vehicle to demonstrate a sound system.

So facing up to the threat of your doomdom (to say nothing of your social security's future), your task is to convince your audience that you can offer him some extras that—at present, just can't be packaged for home consumption. What you offer is visual perception and *live* stereo. You can also offer him quality comparison and togetherness. But most of all, you can offer him *you* in person, in living color, and in un-electric sound.

Of course, I can imagine you're going to have a rough time at first. After all, he's accustomed to twisting a bunch of knobs, selecting his own programs, and listening to the whole thing with his shoes off and maybe even a beer or so.

You may have to get a Foundation Grant to re-design your hall. A few helpful suggestions here would not be out of order, especially since I have probed deeply into the problem and have your interest (as always) at heart.

First of all, tear out all of the old-style seats and put in small cubicles, each of which has a pseudo-control panel with lots of knobs and bunches of small red and green lights. You can install simulated systems that will let him twist dials to his heart's content. Put in a coin-operated beer machine if you like, and let him take off his shoes. And instead of a program or scores for him to look at, provide him with a kit which (if he puts it all together) will turn out to be another kit which, when he puts it all together, turns out to be another kit and so forth and so on. And because what he's going to miss about live music is the sixty-cycle hum, the surface noise, and the record scratch, you can feed this to him over your PA system and finally (as the ultimate in making him feel at home) arrange to have a few odors like overheated tubes and burnt-out transformers piped in through the air vents.

Now, your hall re-designed, you're ready for him to come to your concert. But before you do, plan your programs well. Pick out something with lots of triangles, xylophones, and piccolos in it for the highs, something featuring the tubas and contrabassoons so he'll know your lows are down to par, and get a good stereo effect by using an antiphonal choir or having a sort of question-and-answer piece between the right and left side of your orchestra. What you will pick out for those sitting in the middle has still not yet been determined.

You might even rebuild the stage to represent two huge twin (or "matched") speakers, complete with a grill-cloth cover giving a scrim effect not unlike that of the factory-guaranteed out-of-focus fuzziness of color TV. And oh yes, I did forget one factor in your hall design. Since there is always only one perfect spot to sit when you're listening to stereo (give or take an inch one way or the other), I suggest that all of your seats will have to be one right behind another in a sort of "everybody sitting on the fifty yard line" effect. Of course, the auditorium may end up being one chair wide and three miles long, but you'll have your audience back. In the meanwhile, you can check this theory out by playing your first live-stereo concert in an unused tunnel.

By now you are all looking at each other with sly grins and thinking that old Teach has really flipped his feathers, but a quick glance at the advertising sections of some of our leading magazines will convince you that I am not just having myself a jolly time in jokes and jests. And if you'll pay close attention now, I think this will be the very thing to make you see that it's time that we all joined forces to do something about it.

One company photographed a hi-fi set which stood in front of Carnegie Hall that seemed to ask us "how come you all need Carnegie Hall when you can get our product?" I went by Carnegie Hall the other day and IT was still there, but the set was gone—which will give you some idea of permanent values. Another company advises you that owning their equipment is like bringing the orchestra home with you. Now that alone would keep me from having one because who wants a bunch of oboe players and bass fiddlers to feed? One company advertises that the sound of genius is on their records and another says they have "living sound" (meaning, I guess, that the other company is palming off a bunch of embalmed recently deceased stuff on you, genius or not). But the most sinister of all, I felt, was the advertisement that showed a pretty girl holding a handful of recording tape up to her cheek with this look in her eye that showed the whole world that she was in love with it, reel and all, and didn't care who knew it. Who gets custody of the children—Minnesota Mining?

So no wonder the public who used to go to hear live musicians play Brahms and Beethoven right out loud and without help from an amplifier and nary a tape flutter—no wonder the public has been seduced away from your Hall of Fame and lured into a maze of wires and gadgets and sounds of genius on records and pretty girls in love with magnetic tape and stereo with multiplex on FM and damn near everything else except what you and the composer both want—music.

It is indeed the age of anxiety—at least for your conducting future and in these times of automation, it looks like you're the first to be replaced. If things don't change, you had better get yourself declared a disaster area before poverty goes out of style.

But hark!

There IS hope and be glad you learned it here.

Keep on with what you are doing and don't give up, no matter what. For if worst comes to worst, you can still keep the orchestra live—to hell with the audience. Put *them* on tape!

CHAPTER XIII

From Here To Posterity

In this final chapter (and I already feel like singing the first two verses of Auld Lang Syne), I am sending you out into the world, alone and unguided except for the copy of this book which I hope you will clutch in your hot little hands forever. Don't loan it to anybody, make them buy their own! Let it be your "Koran of Conducting" and consult it every time a new crisis arises. I hope by the time we read those magic words "The End," that we will have covered every nook and cranny of the subject and you will be able to say triumphantly, "We have met the enemy and they are won!" (or something equally triumphant). This last chapter, if I may modestly compare this book to the Bible (which took several people to write, by the way, including the Great Conductor in the Sky), will be for you as Revelations and I hope you memorize it, book, verse, and chapter. According to a friend of mine who read this manuscript in the original foolscap, nothing has been left out of here except a brief mention of the spawning habits of the lamphrey eel and a recipe for fried grits.

Be that as it may, this last chapter endeavors to talk of small but inconsequential things, and the first thing we will talk about are living composers, especially those living near *you*. And this has to do with commissions. You can always spot a composer from about forty paces because he will be bulging a little. This is not contagious, for it is only a score or so that he is carrying around, hoping that he will meet you and that you will notice him and ask to see what makes him

—*your visitor is a clubwoman who has her protege in tow*—.

I've had people ask me to come over to hear their equipment with the same reverent gleam once reserved for viewing th Mona Lisa!

bulgy. Composers follow conductors around like they were trained CID operators, always looking at you with that "yearning-to-be-noticed, and please-oh-please, play-my-masterpiece" attitude. You don't have to actually speak to them, but be nice to them once in awhile and let them lick your hand. Friendly (hopeful) ones are almost equal to ex-opera singers as members of your booster club during concert intermissions.

Let's say that you are going all-out in this matter and either commission a work or hold a contest. There are actually two ways of getting mileage out of the press with composers, and almost either way is fine except that contests are more trouble and the losers are always fretful about it. Besides, unless you want to judge all of the manuscripts yourself, you have to call in a Committee or a Jury, and they're liable to get carried away with something that has five-four time in it and then where are you? Actually a composer doesn't make much money out of a commissioned work, for by the time he pays to have the parts copied, rents a tux, and buys a bus ticket to come and hear it, he might as well have been doing something more lucrative, like spear sharpening. But promise him glory and fame, including his picture in the paper shaking hands with you. Hint somewhere along the line that you may even let him conduct it and he'll fairly slaver with anticipation, and assure him that your pending contract with the disc company—as well as your probable network telecast—will focus sharp attention on his creation and that the least he can expect is a niche in the Hall of Fame.

Commissioning a composer (or even saying you're going to) goes great with the Press who are even more curious about them than they are you. The result will be columns of stuff about the event, especially if you tie-in the name of the town some way in the title. Your opening release to the 4th Estate can read something like this:

> "Maestro Glop announced today that Elmer Whinny, noted American composer living at Lurch, a small farming community twelve miles south of here, has just been commissioned to write a symphonic poem about . . . . (here is inserted the name of the town your orchestra is in)."

There will then follow a short biography of him and a long one of you and how your faith in this man's music has meant so much to him. Secretly hint that you have been helping to pay for his music lessons and have even loaned him a bottle or two of India Ink and a manuscript pen. Your picture will appear with the article, and a lot of folks will get all mixed up and think that not only are you a great conductor, but that you also write symphonic poems on the side.

Be sure to pick out a composer who writes tunes and don't take one of these jokers whose music sounds like a product of an incestuous Univac mating. You want a piece of music with some strong melodies in it so that you can run in "community singing" again on the premiere night and it can turn out to be an "our" song sort of affair with the audience loving every minute of it. If you really want to be safe, use that old program-note bit in which the composer "himself a great admirer of Lincoln, babies, dogs, his mother, and the American flag, incorporates all of these plus a plea for world peace and lowered income taxes in the finale." Somewhere along the way you'll find something that appeals to almost everyone. And then, of course, the name of the Town. This way everybody will remember the name of the piece if they can remember what town it is they live in.

But this sort of thing can be rough on composers. I know one fellow who wrote a piece named "Tulsa" and it was very successful. He then wrote one called "The Son of Tulsa" and still another one called "Tulsa Re-Visited." It was only when he got mixed up and did one entitled "The Son of the Man who wrote Tulsa re-visits Oklahoma City" and then wrapped it up and sent it to a conductor in Amarillo that the whole thing got the best of him and they had to lead him away. The last I heard of him, he was taking shots for it. Some even on the rocks.

This commission routine can be used year after year and is always good for lots of publicity in newspaper and radio, however, you'll have to make the TV appearances alone usually as most composers can hardly afford to write music, let alone get their teeth capped.

Another topic that ties in here with composers is Foundation Grants and there should be some information included here on that, as they are also status symbols which carry all sorts of prestige with them. Foundations are organizations whose main business is having money but not giving it away unless you can talk them out of it. They're supposed to make large scale contributions to the interests of mankind, but they don't if they can help it. It is all mixed up in the tax structure somehow and I don't understand it very clearly or I would get one for myself. All I know is that there are foundations on almost every subject such as "The Fund for Feeding Felines" (cat houses have been established all over the country for this purpose), and those like "The Gerp Family Fund for Old Funds of the Gerp Family." Each of these foundations (some 6,000 of them in the United States) are listed in a book published by another foundation, one of whose main purposes seems to be publishing books about the other foundations.

As you look through this book, you will see that many of them are restricted to giving their money away only for specific purposes in specific areas. Like there might be one in Kentucky which gives money only in one county in Kentucky, and only then in months which have "R" in them. Descendents of people who fought on the losing side in the Whiskey Rebellion are the only ones who need apply. Some of these outfits restrict themselves almost to the point where they won't give anything away except during a monsoon season or if you have some unknown disease like discography. Weed all of these out, for what you are looking for is one that has something to do with the arts in one way or another—and when you find one (and there are several), get an appointment with the executive secretary.

Dress carefully for the occasion. Foundation garments should be neat, but not too prosperous looking. Nothing can get you a turn-down quicker than for you to look better dressed than the executive secretary. When you have waded through the plush carpet into his office, he will want to know what sort of project you have in mind—and in the same breath will tell you that they have given away all of their money until the year three thousand in order to discourage you from hanging around the lobby until they get some more. This is generally a fib, so casually mention your close friendship with one or more members of his Foundation Board. You can say things like:

"L.B.J. told me that what I have in mind really struck him as AOK."
You now have the upper hand because he's not too sure whether you
really do know old L.B.J. or not, so go ahead and describe this grant
you want which will have them supply you with vast gobs of money
in order to bring music to the over-privileged. The under-privileged
have other foundations *they* can go to. You describe the ever-growing
needs, the endless sacrifices on your part to do this for them, and most
of all, point out the amount of newspaper spread HIS foundation
will get if they give you the money. Foundations like to give money
to people who can get them front page stories and they keep scrap
books like crazy.

The first time you go, you won't get any—but if you really do
know L.B.J. and that crowd or have a friend who knows L.B.J. or if
L.B.J. has a friend who wants something from one of your friends,
you'll get your grant and the subsequent newspaper spreads will be
fantastic with the headlines praising both the foundation and you!
And besides, you'll get your picture in the paper because foundations
rarely have a glossy print of themselves. So not only is all of this
worth your effort to get the money, but foundation hopping is fun.
And the over-privileged do appreciate it, after all.

Next to getting foundation grants to raise your local prestige,
doctor's degrees of the honorary kind are hard to beat. No conductor
is really satisfied unless he can be called "doctor," too. And so I will
put in a few ways you can achieve this, if you use your native skill and
ingenuity the way you have been using it to get as far as you've gotten
so far. First, pick yourself a university. Don't go in for these mail-
order types that let you earn your degree legitimately by taking correspondence courses. In the first place, it's hours of tedium and in the
second place, you feel damn foolish going down to the main post
office in a cap and gown to graduate. Pick out a university that has a
good-sounding name that people have heard of. And preferably some
distance from your own community lest word get back concerning the
details of your clandestine negotiations with the Dean of the Music
School who just happens to have written a Symphony No. III (his
Spastic) which you will then play for him, but ONLY after you've
gotten yours first.

Or failing this, pick out a university that needs a stadium and promise to give them one. This may bind you financially for awhile, but you can always get out of it later by throwing yourself on the mercy of the bankruptcy court. Or maybe you can find a stadium that needs a university and you can give them one of those. Better than actually giving, is hinting that you have just come from your soliciter and drawn your will, leaving every farthing to them. Considering the fact that your entire estate at present is an antique set of Grove's Dictionaries and two balloon tires for a 1928 Essex, you don't have much to lose even if you do die and they happen to get it. At least they will call you doctor in your obituary.

And then when you get one, don't stop there. Collect doctorates like debs collect charm bracelets or certain South American tribes collect shrunken heads. Pretty soon you'll have more degrees than a fever thermometer and if they really do put all those "doctors" in front of your name, they'll sound like they're stuttering.

I received an honorary doctorate myself for writing a symphony. My two brothers (who were both legitimate Ph.D.'s) sent me a telegram telling me that I was now the black sheepskin of the family. At first I didn't appreciate my degree since it was just honorary, but some time later I heard of some character who got an earned Ph.D. for writing a thesis on "The origin of the Glomph, a little-known disease found in footnotes for organists similar to Ptomaine," I quit looking down on my own and started making everybody call me doctor, even the nurses. So grab the degree and become a doctor. Just don't take night calls and stay away from infectious diseases like mumps and leprosy. Those are for composers.

Another of our tidbits for this chapter concerns the care and feeding of the assistant conductor. You only start really rating in a town when the board appoints an assistant for you. It isn't necessarily that they think you need help, but they have relatives too. However, if you get to pick your own, quiz him unmercifully and if he looks like he has the possibility of really getting somewhere, don't hire him. Instead, try to get a good pianist who can read your scores through for you while you practice your beats, but who is as awkward as Ichabod Crane and twice as un-coordinated. This way, no matter how keen his insight is into the O'Bryan Overture by von Weber, when he gets up on the podium he will look like Sancho Panzo tilting at wind-mills with himself playing both parts. One way to show yourself to good advantage is to let him conduct for a minute or so when some of the board members drop around and then take the stick away from him. It is the difference between a swan and an albatross. Assistant conductors are good for children's concerts, however, especially open-air ones where it is liable to rain anyway. Whatever you do, insist that at all times he call you "Maestro."

We hinted in a previous chapter about this word but so far we haven't come out much in the open about it. The term "Maestro" is an Italian word (Berlitz, page 9) meaning "Teacher." And it signi-fies that you are just one step higher than the time-beater or "let's all try to stop together once fellows" type of leader when this term is used at you. Although it *would be* legitimate for a sousaphone teacher to use this word for himself, this is usually not the case—and so con-ductors have sort of adopted it for their own use as an accolade or superlative that has all the symbolic meaning of a high priesthood or a six-star general.

Unfortunately, you cannot use "Maestro" and "Doctor" at the same time, just as you cannot (unless you are given to great displays of immodesty) refer to yourself in these terms—although I must admit that using the term "doctor" in front of your own name is great for getting airline reservations. But usually these are privileges re-served for others, plenty of whom are always around and wanting to use them on you so they can tell other folks later about this conversa-tion with the "Maestro" or "Doctor." I personally reserve this par-ticular term "Maestro" altogether for a giant named Toscanini, who, in his own wearing of the mantle, seems to have made it impossible for others to use with any sense of it really fitting them comfortably. So I'd stick to doctor—this way the Mayo Brothers can call you in if they ever get a sick sousaphonist.

A few hints of orchestral decorum during concerts should be inserted here. A lot of those jokers can really distract an audience's attention away from you if you don't watch them. Take fiddle players, for instance. They weave around like dervishes sometimes and do all sorts of attention-getting tricks like dropping their bows or breaking their strings with disconcerting little "ping" noises. I've already warned you about percussion players, but I haven't mentioned the string basses yet. *They* stand up, too, you know. And the mere fact that they're capable of holding one of those heavy things up all evening impresses the average spectator no end. They look like a bunch of magicians trying to saw somebody in half with a dull blade, and they are forever talking to each other during performances. Permit this only if they're asking important questions, like "Where is the place?"

Flute players are always shining up their instruments and spend all of their measures-rest whipping out silk scarves and rubbing and scrubbing like they were polishing the Hope diamond. Make them do this before concerts since a lot of ladies in the audience exude empathy toward this kind of musical housecleaning and sometimes even drop around after concerts to offer suggestions for using Brillo or such. Bassoons are not too bad, although they do stick up sort of high and look a little like unused flag poles at half mast.

One of your big problems are the clarinets. They are never happy and are always swabbing out their instruments with chamois skin. Then they hold them up to the light and peer through them as if they were birdwatchers with short telescopes. And oboe players—well, that fonky blast you hear now and then that sounds like a mallard duck with the croup is an oboe player testing his reed. How George Frederick Handel stood forty of them, I'll never know.

But of all of your fine feathered friends in your musical barnyard, the harpist is the worst scene stealer of all. She comes out about an hour ahead of time tuning it, and then during the concert, flings her arms with every note she plays—looking exactly like an umpire calling a man out at third base. Caution: try not to get a pretty one if you can help it, as the men in the audience will look at her and you'll never be seen at all and besides, their wives will be jealous if her measurements are better than theirs.

To sum up on this subject, give your orchestra a sharp talking-to and tell them that their job is to play and none of that showing off to attract attention. Either that or hypnotize them into a state of flacidity so they'll be putty in your hands. Hypnotized bass players look a little like refugees from Alcoholics Anonymous, however, so don't put them too far under or the critics may write "In the last number we're not too sure what the score was, but we do know that the basses were loaded!"

There's another small last item to insert here which might be called "tempers, fits, and tantrums." More logically this should have been included under the chapter on platform postures and profiles, however, I didn't want you to be confused about such thespianism. Of all the dramatic arts that are available to the man with the baton, stagecraft is the one most needed besides music. And among the elements of good theater is a real whoppin' temper tantrum if things look like they aren't going your way at rehearsals. You can't use these things at concerts much. At concerts all you can do is just make speeches to the audience about your soloists, crying babies, or noisy audiences.

Tempers may be roughly divided into two categories: (a) the slow burn, and (b) the outburst (the latter sounding like the death cry of a wounded bull elephant). The slow burn is sometimes referred to as the "sulk" but it isn't very effective unless you have a large lower lip to let hang petulantly. When you are aroused to such a one of these conditions, let the orchestra know you are angry by ceasing to conduct immediately and doing something distracting like pushing your music stand over. This makes a hell of a racket and even drummers will look up to see what drowned them out. Once you've got their attention, just stand there. Get red in the face if you can. I have a friend who practiced getting red in the face and he could do it any old time he wanted to. He became so successful at it that he was offered a job with the Cherokee Indians and after that would have been a successful stop light in Omaha except he couldn't change to green quick enough to suit the city manager.

Stand up there and let them know you are mad as the devil about something *they've* done. Gasp a little for breath (you can brush up on this by going to a fish market and watching codfish) and look at the orchestra with such contempt as if you just found out they didn't really like you. It is best in these circumstances not to say anything.

Just stand there and cower them with some of your more severe glances and then finally yell "Da Capo!" and give a quick downbeat. To this day most of them won't know what you were mad about and they'll play better out of a combined sense of relief that you didn't think it was them, or if you did, you let them off this time without a public warning.

The more effective of these two forms of temper displays is the roar. Practice roaring at home—at least until you're told not to or asked to move unless you stop doing it after 10 P.M. Better still, get a room near the zoo and you won't bother anyone except maybe the other animals. When the proper occasion arises during rehearsal (never at concerts, now!), roar. But make sure you do this during a soft passage as sometimes full brass has a tendency to be louder than even a conductor. Once you've got their attention and some of the more timid among them may be even cringing a little, roar again. This second roar is not quite as loud, more like you're getting used to the pain of it all. You can stamp your foot some, if you like, but be wary of this unless your other foot is out of the way. Fold your arms across your chest and slowly clench and unclench your knuckles (they're on your hand there) and then give them a speech sounding exactly as if you were on the border-line of apoplexy or had just finished trying to run up seven flights of stairs.

"I—have—never—" (grit your teeth a little if you think they can hear it) "heard—no—never, ever heard—anything so—so—..." Here, shrug your shoulders. At this point you can either walk off the podium in a huff (risking some ambitious assistant conductor finishing the rehearsal for you) or demand a public apology from the entire orchestra, right down to the last bombard, serpent and sackbut. There are a million varients of these devices. Use them freely, but never forget one thing. Don't ever tell them what it is you're angry about. Even if you know yourself.

Well, I see our time is up. We have fought the good fight and finished the course—and just as it has been a great job for me to impart the collective wisdom of career experience to you, so I know that all of this will do you good if you use it well. I hope you haven't minded my fun-loving attitude now and then as a jest or a little witicism crept in, the *more-better* to illustrate a point *with*. Now you are on your own. If you have read this far and understood it, you shouldn't have any trouble with your musicians.

I just know you're all going to be successful, and because of this, my cup runneth over.

Does anybody have a napkin?